ETHICS OF WAR

"Christians are constantly in need of moral reflection about the morality of war. We live in a dangerous world where conflict between nations is inevitable. This volume is an indispensable primer for understanding war that draws from both Scripture and the Christian tradition to help contemporary believers encounter the headlines with wisdom."

—**Daniel Darling**, director of the Land Center for Cultural Engagement, Southwestern Baptist Theological Seminary

"In the aftermath of America's long wars against terrorism and in the midst of wars and rumors of wars all around us, Paul Miller offers young students and seminarians a useful introductory text on the Christian tradition of just war. Miller is part of an important resurgence in faithful, confident, and even muscular Christian reflection on human conflict. At numerous points—especially in his accounts of military necessity, proportionality, and discrimination, and in his case studies on Ukraine and the Israeli-Hamas war—Miller is unafraid to speak uncomfortable truths that sometimes cut against popular sentiment. Accessible, engaging, and succinct, covering a range of important subjects—natural law, justice, sovereignty, the moral care of veterans and their families, new technologies, and many others—*Ethics of War* will launch interested students to new areas of deeper research in this rich and vital tradition."

—**Marc LiVecche**, McDonald Distinguished Scholar on Ethics, War, and Public Life at *Providence: A Journal of Christianity & American Foreign Policy* and non-resident research scholar at the US Naval War College

"Paul Miller's *Ethics of War* is simply excellent. It ably pulls together biblical, theological, and philosophical arguments to explain, defend, and apply the Christian just war tradition. Christians and others interested in navigating well the terrible dilemmas of war will find themselves well served by this book."

—**Bryan McGraw**, professor of politics and dean of natural and social sciences, Wheaton College

"If the peacemakers are the blessed ones, as Jesus said, is any war ever right? If so, when and how? These questions were complicated enough for two thousand years of debate within Christianity. Now, with nuclear and biological weaponry, drone warfare, and artificial intelligence, the questions are even harder. No one is better equipped to guide Christians through seeking and finding the right direction on war and peace than Paul Miller. This book will help you as you seek to conform your conscience to the kingdom of Christ."

—**Russell Moore**, editor-in-chief, *Christianity Today*

"Paul Miller's *Ethics of War* is a superb, biblically based book that should be used in our churches and classrooms. Miller writes in a clear and accessible style, providing a prudent, theologically sound approach to issues of peace, justice, and security. Miller rightfully notes that both the Old and New Testaments call for virtuous leaders to serve, protect, defend, and promote the common good in a fallen world, and he provides us with a rich view of Christian statecraft for our times."

—**Eric Patterson**, president and CEO, Victims of Communism Memorial Foundation, and author of *A Basic Guide to the Just War Tradition*

"Paul Miller is a scholar uniquely equipped by background and conviction to address the ethics of war. He is a leader in the renaissance of just war scholarship. In our world of renewed great power competition and proxy wars, his insights are timely and needed."

—**Mark Tooley**, president, Institute for Religion and Democracy, and editor-in-chief, *Providence* magazine

"As both a scholar of just war theory and a practitioner of just war, given his training and career, Paul Miller is in the unique position to speak with an authority that few can on a subject. I warmly commend *Ethics of War* as a faithful primer on one of the most important contributions of Christian thought to ancient and modern ethical theory. Readers will benefit from the faithful fusion of biblical argumentation and natural law principles as well as the pastoral guidance on caring for soldiers."

—**Andrew T. Walker**, associate professor of Christian ethics and public theology, The Southern Baptist Theological Seminary, and fellow, The Ethics and Public Policy Center

ESSENTIALS *in Christian Ethics*

ETHICS OF WAR

A Short Companion

Paul D. Miller

editors
C. Ben Mitchell & Jason Thacker

ACADEMIC®
BRENTWOOD, TENNESSEE

Ethics of War: A Short Companion

Published by B&H Academic®
Brentwood, Tennessee

ISBN: 978-1-0877-7012-3

Dewey Decimal Classification: 241
Subject Heading: CHRISTIAN ETHICS \ THEOLOGY \ ETHICS

Cover design by Emily Keafer Lambright. Cover illustration by J614/iStock.

Printed in the United States of America

30 29 28 27 26 25 VP 1 2 3 4 5 6 7 8 9 10

CONTENTS

SERIES PREFACE

In 1876, German Lutheran theologian Christoph Ernst Luthardt eloquently illustrated the relationship between theology and ethics. He wrote, "God first loved us is the summary of Christian doctrine. We love Him is the summary of Christian morality."[1] The wedding of theology and ethics was later embraced by generations of theologians and ethicists, such as Protestant titans Herman Bavinck and Carl F. H. Henry,[2] who rightly understood the primacy of both theology and ethics in the Christian life. But at times in the recent history of the Protestant church, the study of ethics has been relegated to a mere application of theology and biblical studies rather than understood as a first-order discipline in rich partnership with the theological task.

The aim of the Christian ethic can be summed up in the words of Jesus in Matt 22:37–39. We, God's people, are to "love the Lord

---

[1] Christoph Ernst Luthardt, *Apologetic Lectures on the Moral Truths of Christianity*, trans. Sophia Taylor (Edinburgh: T&T Clark, 1876), 26.

[2] See Herman Bavinck, *Reformed Ethics*, ed. John Bolt, vol. 1, *Created, Fallen, and Converted Humanity* (Grand Rapids: Baker, 2019), §1:58; and Carl F. H. Henry, *Christian Personal Ethics*, 2nd ed. (Grand Rapids: Baker, 1979), 486.

[our] God with all [our] heart[s] and with all [our] soul[s] and with all [our] mind[s] . . . and to love [our] neighbor as [ourselves]." We hear echoes of this summation in the words of Luthardt, Bavinck, and Henry, each of whom spoke of how God's people are to love him as the summary of Christian morality. Thus, Christian ethics is nothing less than a primary motivation for those seeking to be faithful to God in all of life and live in light of how he has revealed himself in Scripture. Ethics as discipleship is a key theme throughout Scripture and one the church must elevate as we seek God's face in the academy, in our churches, and especially in our personal lives as transformed creatures made in the very image of God.

While Christian ethics is a core element of God's revelation to his people about how they are to live as his followers, it is also a distinct philosophical discipline that must be studied in consideration of the rich history of moral thought seen throughout the life of the church and the wider society. Much of today's discourse about Christian ethics tends to focus on the mere application of theological or philosophical principles, rather than understanding how these principles have been derived and refined over time in light of the massive metaphysical and epistemological shifts in the history of thought.

Given the recent tendency in wider evangelicalism at times to downplay the direct study of ethics in our curricula, in our church life, and in the task of discipleship, the Essentials in Christian Ethics series is designed to illuminate the richness of the Christian ethic, as well as how ethics is intricately woven into the whole of the Christian life. We have gathered renowned ethicists and leading figures in their fields of theological and philosophical inquiry who are passionate about proclaiming the biblical ethic to a world desperately in need of Christ.

The series is made up of short, introductory volumes spanning metaethics, normative ethics, and applied ethics. Each volume can be used independently as an introduction to the crucial elements of the Christian ethical tradition, including resources for further reading and key concepts for those seeking to dig deeper into the beauty of God's revelation. They can also be used as supplements to a larger ethics curriculum, where a specialized volume could be used to augment a primary text or to give deeper insight into particular contemporary ethical debates.

As editors, we have longed for a series like this to be written by scholars who understand and apply the rich relationship of theology and ethics in their teaching, writings, and ministry. This series is designed to model for readers how the biblical ethic applies to every area of life both as a distinct theological and philosophical discipline in the context of the Christian moral tradition from a robust Protestant viewpoint. We pray this serves the wider academy, those training in our colleges and seminaries, and especially those seeking to employ the riches of Christian ethics in the context of the local church.

C. Ben Mitchell and Jason Thacker
Series Editors

PREFACE

In 2021 I published *Just War and Ordered Liberty*, the fruit of two decades of reflection on justice and war. The book is a work of intellectual history, political theory, and international relations. I traced the evolution of the just war traditions across millennia of evolution, argued for a new synthesis, and applied my argument to contemporary security challenges. The book was written for advanced undergraduate and graduate students in the aforementioned fields and was responding to the need for a new direction in just war scholarship.

Having finished that work, I recognized another need to which this new book is a response. This book is written for pastors, seminarians, chaplains, military officers, national security decision-makers, and undergraduates new to the field of study—audiences who need something more accessible, more immediate, and more usable. I hope this book takes my main arguments from the earlier work and turns them into something practical for those who make decisions about war, those who go to war, and those who shepherd the warriors. At the same time, I have gone further than the last book in laying out the scriptural foundations of the Augustinian just war tradition and something like a biblical theology of war.

This book reuses or reprints portions of some of my previous writing with permission: *Just War and Ordered Liberty*, "What Does a Just End to the Russo-Ukraine War Look Like?," "Ordered Liberty in the Bible," "Israel vs. Hamas: A Just War Analysis," and "To Stand with the Palestinians, Support Israel Against Hamas."

I would like to thank Jason Thacker and C. Ben Mitchell for giving me the opportunity to contribute to the Essentials in Christian Ethics series with B&H Academic®.

1

The Bible and Warfare

What does the Bible say about war? Quite a lot, actually: the Bible is bloody, replete with war, murder, death, fighting, and battle. Depending on how we count, the Old Testament records eighty-nine battles, fifteen rebellions, and eighteen assassinations.[1] Biblical authors use war as a metaphor for judgment and trials, for the struggle against sin, for the apocalypse—and, surprisingly, for the character of God himself. War was so common that adulthood was defined as being of military age: when Israel recorded its census in the book of Numbers, it recorded "every male twenty years old or more, everyone who could serve in the army" (1:20).

[1] For a list of battles, see "Every Battle in the Bible," *Constantly Reforming* (blog), accessed April 4, 2024, https://constantlyreforming.wordpress.com/every-battle-in-the-bible/. For a list of rebellions, see "Old Testament Rebellions," *Bible and Prayer Square,* updated August 5, 2013, https://web.archive.org/web/20201027103715/https://sites.google.com/site/bibleandprayersquare/rebellions/old-testament-rebellions.

Solomon counsels us to "wage war with sound guidance" (Prov 20:18), but the prophets warn against the man who has war "in his heart" (Ps 55:21). God commands Israel to wage war in the Old Testament yet denies King David's request to build the temple because he is a "man of war" (1 Chron 28:3). God promises to deliver his people from the scourge of war and, in some of the most moving descriptions of the new creation, promises to put an end to war forever. Perhaps perfectly capturing the Bible's seeming ambiguity on the subject, Solomon reminds us that there is "a time for war and a time for peace" (Eccl 3:8).

What should we think of war? What guidance does the Bible give us for praising or condemning, participating in or protesting, war? War is sadly common throughout history and around the world. Christians have been constantly confronted with the question of whether and to what extent they can support or serve in war in good conscience. They are also left with the task of deciding to what extent they are obligated to oppose war, even at the cost of ridicule, suspicion, arrest, imprisonment, or execution. Today, most citizens in the developed world have not experienced political violence—a historical rarity and an incredible blessing—but as taxpaying citizens in democratic countries that fund large, standing armies, we still have a responsibility for thinking carefully about how those armies are used.[2]

We are fortunate that God has blessed the church with a long tradition of reflection on these questions. Rooted in the biblical

---

[2] The "developed world" is the polite way of referring to rich countries, compared to the relatively poor nations of what used to be called the third world. The thirty-seven member states of the Organization for Economic Cooperation and Development is an approximate map of the developed world.

text, theologians throughout church history have offered answers to the questions of war. Over time, a mainstream consensus emerged and cohered into a discrete theological tradition: the just war tradition. The just war tradition stands in contrast to other theological options including pacifism, which holds that war is never justified, and holy war, which claims that war should be waged to spread Christianity by force and to kill its opponents. The just war tradition is also distinct from the secular tradition of realism, which holds that war is self-justifying and needs no moral framework other than political necessity to guide its use.

The just war tradition is distinct from pacifism because it holds that war may sometimes be justified, even obligatory. It is distinct from realism by insisting that, though war may be permissible, it must be justified by a moral framework of justice and peace, not the raw pursuit of power or political convenience. It is also distinct from holy war by insisting that the causes for which war must be fought should be tied to the common good, not to the parochial interests of the church. Just war is an instrument to be used by a legitimately constituted government, which has responsibility for all citizens of all faiths, to uphold justice and peace in the face of violent assault.

Pacifism

Many Christians are intuitively drawn to pacifism: principled opposition to violence in all forms for any reason. We have absorbed the King James Version (KJV) of the sixth commandment, which instructs "Thou shalt not kill" (Exod 20:13). Jesus commands us to love our enemies, tells us not to resist an evildoer, and exhorts us to turn the other cheek (Matt 5:39, 44). The plain and simple wording of these passages seems to imply that we should not kill other people even if they are trying to kill us. War, even in self-defense, involves killing other human beings made in the image of God. How can we love them at the same time that we kill them? Especially if killing them might mean sending them to hell?

This is why many of the early church fathers (e.g., Tertullian and Origen) counseled pacifism and why much of the early church was (from what we know) largely pacifist.[3] Today churches in the Quaker, Amish, Mennonite, and Brethren traditions continue to preach pacifism (many influenced by the writings of Stanley Hauerwas and John Howard Yoder).[4] I have found that many younger Christians default to an instinctive pacifism in the absence of any teaching to the contrary, unaware that pacifism has been a minority viewpoint for most of the church's history—though they also instinctively reject pacifism when asked how to respond to genocide, terrorism, or invasion. There are no pacifists in the face of the Holocaust.

The Bible does not command us to be pacifists though. The KJV mistranslated the sixth commandment. Most English translations correctly render the commandment to prohibit "murder" not "killing." The Hebrew word used in Exod 20:13 is *retzach*, which specifically means "unlawful killing" (and also "manslaughter" or "causing death through negligence"). "The term used in the commandment

---

[3] See Knut Willem Ruyter, "Pacifism and Military Service in the Early Church," *CrossCurrents* 32, no. 1 (1982): 54–70. See also Ronald H. Bainton, "The Early Church and War," *Harvard Theological Review* 39, no. 3 (1946): 189–212.

[4] See, for example, Stanley Hauerwas, *War and the American Difference: Theological Reflections on Violence and National Identity* (Grand Rapids: Baker Academic, 2011); John Howard Yoder, *Nevertheless: The Varieties and Shortcomings of Religious Pacifism* (Huntingdon, IN: Herald, 1992). Hauerwas is among the most prominent theologians influenced by the Anabaptist tradition today. Yoder was a leading voice in the Mennonite tradition before his death in 1997.

is the specific one to denote what we call murder . . . [the] violent, wilful [*sic*], malicious assault upon the life of another," according to John Murray.[5] Other scholars have noted that "this verb is never used in the [Old Testament] of killing in war" or of judicial execution.[6] A typical passage involving *retzach* is Ps 94:6: "They kill the widow and the resident alien and murder the fatherless." Lawful killing—killing done under law by legitimate authority for a justified, public purpose, including self-defense, policing, judicial execution, and war—is not *retzach* and is not included in the sixth commandment.

Other biblical passages support the idea that war is not prohibited by the sixth commandment. For example, Abram's participation in the War of the Ten Kings in Genesis 14 to rescue Lot is not presented as sinful; rather, the priest Melchizedek pronounces Abram's victory a blessing from God: "Abram is blessed by God Most High, Creator of heaven and earth, and blessed be God Most High who has handed over your enemies to you" (Gen 14:19–20).

Similarly, the same God who prohibited *retzach* also commanded Israel to go to war to take the land of Canaan. Though we understand Israel's war-making authority is not a model for us today (more on this below), it nonetheless illustrates that the original audience of Exodus 20 did not understand the sixth commandment to prohibit killing in authorized combat. God also authorized the death penalty for a range of crimes. Neither the death penalty nor killing in combat are described as *retzach* and are not prohibited by the sixth commandment. God would not prohibit and command the same thing.

---

[5] John Murray, *Principles of Conduct: Aspects of Biblical Ethics* (Grand Rapids: Eerdmans, 1957), 113.

[6] See *ESV Study Bible* (Wheaton, IL: Crossway, 2008), note on Deut 5:17.

In several passages (Exod 15:3; Isa 42:13), the Bible speaks of God as a "man of war" (ESV). This is another suggestion that the Bible does not command pacifism. The biblical authors would not use something intrinsically evil as a metaphor to teach about God's character. God is never said to be a murderer, a prostitute, a slanderer, or a blasphemer. He is described as a shepherd, a rock, an eagle, a father—and a warrior. Though war is a bad thing in many respects, there is something about it that nonetheless reflects God's character. How could we understand the metaphor without direct experience of things said to be like God? And how could there be anything about the experience akin to God's character unless there was something about it that could be praiseworthy?

In the New Testament, when Roman soldiers asked John the Baptist what they needed to do to repent and be saved, he did not tell them to leave the army. Rather, he told them not to abuse their authority, implying such authority was, in principle, legitimate: "And he said to them, 'Don't take money from anyone by force or by false accusation, and be satisfied with your wages'" (Luke 3:14). If they accept their wages, they accept the duty for which they are being paid—a duty that included the use of force—and John implicitly affirmed the legitimacy of both. When Jesus and Paul interacted with Roman soldiers and centurions (Matthew 8, Acts 10, Acts 21–23, Acts 27), they similarly never suggested that the soldiers were sinning by virtue of being a soldier. Jesus clearly proclaims that the centurion of Matthew 8 exhibited saving faith, even while still serving as a centurion. Jesus's disciples had swords on hand, suggesting Jesus never prohibited their possession, and Jesus even commanded his disciples to buy them, presumably for self-defense (Luke 22:36).

How, then, do we understand Jesus's command to love our enemies and turn the other cheek? First, we should note that Jesus himself used violence to drive the money changers out of the temple with a whip (John 2:13–22), an act that did not involve killing but must be kept in mind when we interpret his words about loving enemies: love and physical force are not necessarily opposites. Using force to stop the sinner from his sin is a loving act. As Augustine argued a few centuries later, "When, however, men are prevented, by being harmed, from doing wrong, it may be said that a real service is done to themselves. . . . For in the correction of a son, even with some sternness, there is assuredly no diminution of a father's love . . . The person from whom is taken away the freedom which he abuses in doing wrong is vanquished with benefit to himself."[7] We are commanded to love both our neighbors and our enemies. When our enemy attacks our neighbor, we love them both by defending one against the other, not by standing by passively.

As for not resisting an evildoer, the answer has to do with the difference between *individual* and *institutional* authority. God ordained specific *institutions*, each with distinct authorities, responsibilities, and powers. Understanding the specific institutional authority of government is crucial to recognizing its authority to use force that individuals lack. Jonathan Leeman helpfully reminds us to recognize the presence of institutions in Scripture. Drawing from scholarship on institutions, he defines them as "'behavior shaping rule structures' or 'the rules of a game in society.'" God created the "behavior shaping rule structure" of marriage, for example, a fundamental institution to human life. Leeman adds that to speak of "rules" means that institutions shape behavior according to a standard of right and wrong: "institutions are the application of

[7] Quoted in Herbert A. Deane, *The Political and Social Ideas of St. Augustine* (New York: Columbia Univ. Press, 1963), 164–65.

authority to a relationship."[8] God created the law code of Israel and a government to enforce it, and a religious code with a priestly class to enact it. Institutions embody authority to shape human life and make us behave in some ways rather than other ways.

God has authorized institutions to do things that individuals may not do. For example, throughout Scripture, God gives specific commands to kings and priests—and the institutions they govern—that do not apply to individuals. An individual without God-ordained institutional authority who tries to act like a king is a usurper, such as Absalom (2 Samuel 15–18) and Adonijah (1 Kings 1), and they were justly punished. Similarly, those who try to mediate worship of God—to act like priests—without the institutional authority to do so are sinning, as when Saul tried to usurp the priests' powers (1 Samuel 13) or when the priests acted outside their authority to worship false gods (Aaron and the golden calf in Exodus 32) or when the priests worshiped the true God in the wrong way (Aaron's sons offering unauthorized fire in Leviticus 10).

God created institutions and commissioned them with specific authorities and responsibilities. This is the key to harmonizing Jesus's command not to resist an evildoer with biblical passages about the role of government. God created the institution of government and gave it legitimate authority to uphold earthly justice and peace. That authority comes with permission to use force—permission not granted to individuals. Paul writes in the cornerstone text for any discussion of war:

> Let everyone submit to the governing authorities, since there is no authority except from God, and the authorities

---

[8] Quoted in Jonathan Leeman, *Political Church: The Local Assembly as Embassy of Christ's Rule* (Downers Grove, IL: InterVarsity, 2016), 107, 111.

> that exist are instituted by God. So then, the one who resists the authority is opposing God's command, and those who oppose it will bring judgment on themselves. For rulers are not a terror to good conduct, but to bad. Do you want to be unafraid of the one in authority? Do what is good, and you will have its approval. For it is God's servant for your good. But if you do wrong, be afraid, because it does not carry the sword for no reason. For it is God's servant, an avenger that brings wrath on the one who does wrong. Therefore, you must submit, not only because of wrath but also because of your conscience. And for this reason you pay taxes, since the authorities are God's servants, continually attending to these tasks. Pay your obligations to everyone: taxes to those you owe taxes, tolls to those you owe tolls, respect to those you owe respect, and honor to those you owe honor. (Rom 13:1–7)

In strikingly vivid language, Paul argues that God gave government a sword and permission to use it. Jesus tells individuals not to resist an evildoer, but Paul commands sword-bearing rulers to bring terror to evildoers. That sounds like a contradiction until we recognize that how we react to evildoers depends on whether we are acting as individual citizens or as rulers. Should rulers not resist evildoers? They would be derelict in their duties: God *commands* government to resist evildoers. Should individuals run around with swords bringing people to justice? That would make them vigilantes, criminals themselves subject to the government's sword (Marvel's *Avengers*, sadly, lacks biblical authority). Jesus is speaking to individuals, Paul to institutions. In Matthew 5, Jesus is not speaking to rulers or offering guidance about how government is supposed to respond to crime, violence, disorder, or invasion.

Individuals should turn the other cheek, but they can also call the police to arrest the man who hit them.

The early church fathers' pacifism may have been, in part, poor biblical exegesis. Early Christian doctrine could be surprisingly fluid and heterodox. For example, many of the early church fathers held views on the Trinity and Christology that were not always consistent with what eventually came to be recognized as orthodox doctrine at the ecumenical councils in the fourth and fifth centuries.[9] We should be unsurprised, then, if the early church fathers also got some aspects of political theology and their doctrine of civil government wrong, and we should extend some grace to their errors while not allowing ourselves to be confined by them. The pacifism of the early church fathers may also have been a response to specific circumstances in Imperial Rome. The Roman Empire became more explicitly pagan and idolatrous after the first century as emperors claimed divinity and incorporated pagan religious rituals into civic life and military service. Serving in the Roman military might have been sinful because it required pagan idolatry, not because it required physical force.[10]

Tertullian, for example, argues against Christians serving in the Roman army because it involved wearing a laurel of victory (associated in paganism with Apollo and Bacchus). But Tertullian also condemns military service itself, apart from Roman paganism. "Shall it be held lawful to make an occupation of the sword, when the Lord proclaims that he who uses the sword shall perish by the

---

[9] See John Norman Davidson Kelly, *Early Christian Doctrines* (London: A&C Black, 2000).

[10] And the early Christians were not, in fact, unanimously pacifist. See John F. Shean, *Soldiering for God: Christianity and the Roman Army*, vol. 61 (Boston: Brill, 2010).

sword?" he asks, "And shall he apply the chain, and the prison, and the torture, and the punishment, who is not the avenger even of his own wrongs?" Tertullian implicitly invokes Jesus's command to turn the other cheek to argue that Christians cannot act in any capacity that requires physical force, not recognizing the difference between individual and institutional authority. He appeals to Paul's proscription against personal vengeance in Romans 12 without noting Paul's commission to government to act as God's avenger in the very next chapter. He notes that Jesus and Peter recognized the faith of centurions but asserts (without evidence in the biblical text) that soldiers who find faith must then leave the profession of arms.[11]

Today, some individuals feel conscience-bound not to participate in any act of violence. I think there is room to recognize and respect individual conscientious objection to serving in the military—think of Paul's exhortation in Romans 14 to tolerate different conscientious judgments on disputed issues. Many of my ancestors, who came from the Amish and Mennonite traditions, made that choice. I am grateful they lived in a country that allowed them the freedom to make that choice, and I admire the strength of their principled conviction. I made a different choice and served in the US Army during the war in Afghanistan.

However, while we can respect such individual decisions, there is no room to deny on principle the legitimacy of the state and its sword. Pacifism may be an allowable individual choice, but it is not an available option for the government, including for Christians who serve in government. Government exists to uphold order and justice in a fallen world in which sinful humanity seeks to do evil with violent force. Institutional pacifism—a policy by the government never

---

[11] Tertullian, *De Corona*, chap. 11. https://www.logoslibrary.org/tertullian/crown/11.html.

to use force—would be an immoral dereliction of duty, a sin of omission, and a failure to carry out the commission God gave to government. Christians should recognize and, for the most part, support the government's right to use its power to uphold order and justice (with some exceptions, as I discuss in later chapters). If we should not pass judgment on conscientious objectors if they refuse to serve in the military, they should not pass judgment on those who do serve.

Holy War

If government is allowed to use force, why not use it to spread the gospel? Though few make this argument today because it so clearly goes against our contemporary understanding of religious freedom and the legitimate uses of force, it is worth rehearsing the argument because it highlights the importance of institutional authorities that is crucial for the just war tradition. In fact, much of the just war tradition arose in explicit opposition to holy war arguments.

The Bible seems to give us a clear precedent for using force in God's service. God commanded Israel to take the Promised Land by conquest: "However, you must not let any living thing survive among the cities of these people the Lord your God is giving you as an inheritance. You must completely destroy them—the [Hittite], Amorite, Canaanite, Perizzite, Hivite, and Jebusite—as the Lord your God has commanded you, so that they won't teach you to do all the detestable acts they do for their gods, and you sin against the Lord your God" (Deut 20:16–18).

Joshua later implemented God's command after the battle of Jericho: "They completely destroyed everything in the city with the sword—every man and woman, both young and old, and every ox, sheep, and donkey" (Josh 6:21). God did not stop authorizing war once Israel had taken the land: later, in war against the

Hagrites, the tribes of Israel were victorious "because it was God's battle" (1 Chron 5:22). To "devote to destruction" (Exod 22:20 ESV) meant to devote the spoils to God, to destroy them as an act of worship akin to how Israel killed and burned animals in the temple. Israel's soldiers were under orders to purge the land, remove temptation, and worship God by killing everyone.

Though this book is not about theodicy (a theological explanation of evil and vindication of God's goodness), it is worth addressing the obvious concern these passages raise: many readers are bothered by God commanding genocide. But these passages are not different, on their face, from God wiping out humanity by the great flood in Genesis 6–9; God authorizing other wars on a small, non-genocidal scale; or God killing Aaron's sons or Ananias and Saphira for individual sins. If God is the rightful creator and judge of all, he has the authority to take human life. The real question of these passages is not "How could God kill?" but "Should we do the same?"[12]

These wars are not a model for us today because Israel was a unique institution, neither akin to our modern states nor the New Testament church. Israel was both a worldly nation with a government authorized to use force and also God's chosen instrument for revealing his character and unfolding his plan of redemption. Israel enjoyed a unique relationship to God with specific institutional authorities not replicated by any other entity in history.

Other states are, like Israel, governments commissioned to uphold order and earthly justice and may use force to do so. But they lack Israel's commission to embody God's character, mediate right worship of himself, or execute his plan of redemption. Even within Israel, God enforced distinct authorities, separating the roles

[12] For a fuller discussion, see Susan Niditch, *War in the Hebrew Bible: A Study in the Ethics of Violence* (New York: Oxford Univ. Press, 1995).

of priest, prophet, and king, diffusing power in a way unusual in the ancient Near East. God enforced this separation stringently, punishing King Saul when he overstepped his bounds and assumed the functions of the priesthood (1 Samuel 13). If God was careful to separate religious from civil authority in Israel, other governments that do not have Israel's religious commission lack, to a much larger extent, authority to use force for religious ends.

On the other hand, the church in the New Testament era, like Israel in the Old Testament, enjoys religious authority, but it lacks Israel's right to use force. Jesus gave Peter and the apostles the keys to the kingdom of heaven with authority to bind and loose on heaven and earth (Matt 16:19)—that is, to preach the gospel, embody God's character, and enforce discipline within the body of Christ. But the church is not a government and has no commission to use force. Jesus tells us that "my kingdom is not of this world" (John 18:36) and told his disciples to put away their swords—not to endorse pacifism but to indicate that his kingdom is not established by such means. The church is separate from worldly authority, and his servants do not have the tools that worldly authority brings.[13]

That is why there is no hint of Jesus, the apostles, or the early church using compulsion to spread the gospel in the New Testament. Despite later history of some Christian kings using force to spread the gospel, there is no mandate in Scripture for doing do. God uses the convicting power of the Holy Spirit working through the proclamation of evangelists and the loving power of good works to bring his people to him. One of the earliest Christian writings after the New Testament, the "Epistle of Mathetes to Diognetus," emphasizes the point. Did God send Christ "for the purpose of exercising tyranny, or of inspiring fear and terror? By no means, but

[13] See chapters 5–6 in Leeman, *Political Church*.

under the influence of clemency and meekness . . . for violence [or compulsion] has no place in the character of God."[14]

Realism

Governments are authorized to use force, but not in order to spread the gospel. What is government for, then? Under what conditions may it use force? The just war tradition is the mainstream Christian answer, but it will be helpful first to consider a final tradition of thought, one that has dominated much of secular thinking about war: the tradition of realism.[15] For realists, as Thucydides memorably put it in *The Peloponnesian War*, "the strong do what they can, and the weak suffer what they must."[16] According to realism, there is no particular law governing the behavior of states other than the law of the jungle: survival of the fittest. "Our opinion of

[14] "The Epistle of Mathetes to Diognetus," in *Ante-Nicene Fathers*, ed. Alexander Roberts, James Donaldson, and A. Cleveland Coxe, vol. 1 (1885; repr., Eugene, OR: Wipf and Stock, 2022).

[15] Secular, academic realism is distinct from Christian Realism of the kind articulated by twentieth-century theologian Reinhold Niebuhr. Niebuhr recognized the inescapable realities of power politics but insisted that we nonetheless strive for justice within the constraints of what is possible. Christian Realism is the broader theological framework within which the Christian just war tradition stands. See Reinhold Niebuhr, *The Irony of American History* (Chicago: Univ. of Chicago Press, 2008).

[16] Thucydides probably meant his dialogue as a critique of the ruthless amoralism he puts in the mouths of the Athenians, but later realists have simply taken it at face value. See Thucydides, *History of the Peloponnesian War*, trans. Richard Crawley, Project Gutenberg, 2003. https://www.gutenberg.org/files/7142/7142-h/7142-h.htm. A more modern translation puts it somewhat less poetically: "The strong do what they have the power to do and the weak accept what they have to accept," trans. Rex Warner, ed. M. I. Finley (New York: Penguin, 1954), 402.

the gods and our knowledge of men lead us to conclude that it is a general and necessary law of nature to rule whatever one can," the Athenians say in Thucydides's account, "This is not a law that we made ourselves, nor were we the first to act upon it when it was made. We found it already in existence, and we shall leave it to exist for ever among those who come after us."[17]

Similarly, the sixteenth-century Italian diplomat and author Niccolò Machiavelli would counsel princes to "learn how not to be good, and to use this knowledge and not use it, according to the necessity of the case." This was so because "how we live is so far removed from how we ought to live, that he who abandons what is done for what ought to be done, will rather learn to bring about his own ruin than his preservation."[18] If we wish to live within the world as it really is, we cannot afford the luxury of moral scruple.

In the next century, Thomas Hobbes, a British political theorist, argued that "I put for a general inclination of all mankind, a perpetual and restless desire of power after power, that ceaseth only in death."[19] Because of this truth of human nature, humans are either consigned to endless war or compelled to cede their authority to an all-powerful state, a "Mortal God," in terror of which they would be cowed into peaceable order—but only if they held the state in such regard as to make its actions the standard of right and wrong. For Hobbes, the state is literally incapable of committing injustice because if the state did it, it is definitionally not unjust.[20]

---

[17] Thucydides, *History*, 404–5.

[18] Niccolo Machiavelli, *The Prince*, trans. Luigi Ricci (New York: New American Library, 1952), 84.

[19] Thomas Hobbes, *Leviathan*, ed. Edwin Curley (Indianapolis: Hackett, 1994), 58.

[20] Hobbes, 109, 112–13.

Later European history would evolve this into the doctrine of *raison d'état*, or "the reason of state," the idea that policy is self-justifying, that the pursuit of power needs no justification outside itself.

This kind of realism continues to exert influence in the academic discipline of international relations and among some policymakers around the world. But it is important to recognize that while this kind of realism purports to be a mere *description* of how political life really is, it subtly turns into a *prescription* for how statesmen and policymakers should act. It's a dog-eat-dog world (description), which means if you want to survive, you should eat them before they eat you (prescription). Realism counsels us to act without reference to morality.

Realism, in this sense, is not a value-neutral description of the world. It is an ideology cloaked in the language of "reality" as a biased framing device to make it look natural, truthful, hard-nosed, no-nonsense, and data-driven while its opponents are supposedly the opposite and therefore dangerous. Realism is principled opposition to moral aspiration in politics, which is self-contradictory on its face. Any principled case for anything rests on some idea of morality. Realism amounts to opposition to "conventional" morality in the name of "realist" morality.

Realists claim that conventional moral aspiration is dangerous because it is "unrealistic," that is, it cuts against the grain of reality. Going against reality or trying to change other people's beliefs or behavior is always difficult, often impossible, and inevitably costly and risky. Realists advocate the path of least resistance: go with the grain of reality for a low-cost, low-opposition foreign policy. Realism uses its rhetorical trappings to try to convince us that moral aspiration is dangerous and that we should instead accept that the pursuit of national power is the proper, unquestioned goal of international politics.

As I have explored elsewhere, "realism" is a bad description of reality. Humans are moral creatures; it takes practiced effort to think amorally. In that light, we are justified in asking if "realism" is actually a good guide to action.[21] More to the point for this book, we also have to ask if realism is consistent with what the Bible says about the purpose and role of government. Some Christians have, perhaps unconsciously, absorbed a functional kind of realism and argue that the truly moral thing to do is avoid any hint of political moralizing which, they believe, will only lead to foolish utopianism and self-destruction. But as we will see below and in chapter 2, God gives government a specific commission to pursue: not its own power at all costs, but peace, justice, and order—which are moral ideals—or what we might call the conditions of flourishing for the common good. Insofar as realism neglects the pursuit of peace, justice, or order, it is inconsistent with the just war tradition and with a biblical understanding about the purpose of government.

What the Bible Says about War

If the Bible does not condone pacifism, holy war, or realism, what, then, does it say about war?

War Is One of the Chief Evils in the Bible

Outside the conquest narrative, war by men against men is presented almost entirely as a great evil. God used the Babylonian invasion and conquest of 586 BC as the ultimate punishment for

---

[21] See Paul Miller, "The Unreality of Realism in International Relations," H-DIPLO | ISSF Essay 49, October 2, 2019. https://issforum.org/essays/49-realism.

Judah's repeated apostasy. The prophets describe war as a punishment for idolatry (Judg 5:8) and self-reliance (Hos 10:14). In the book of Judges, war is presented as a trial or test: "These are the nations the Lord left in order to test all those in Israel who had experienced none of the wars in Canaan. This was to teach the future generations of the Israelites how to fight in battle, especially those who had not fought before" (Judg 3:1–2). The prolonged suffering of war was a way to remind Israel of its dependency on God.

A spirit of war is closely associated with sin. The psalmist prays for deliverance against the betraying friend: "My friend acts violently against those at peace with him; he violates his covenant. His buttery words are smooth, but war is in his heart. His words are softer than oil, but they are drawn swords" (Ps 55:20–21). "War is in his heart" could be a reference to someone of combative temperament or, more literally, someone who secretly plans for and delights in physical violence. Similarly, Proverbs likens deceit to a weapon of war: "A person giving false testimony against his neighbor is like a war club, a sword, or a sharp arrow" (Prov 25:18). In these passages, war is placed directly alongside lying, manipulation, and betrayal as an example or image of wickedness and evil.

The psalmists pled for God to deliver them from war and praised him for his power to overcome war: "Oppose my opponents, Lord; fight those who fight me" (Ps 35:1); "Trample underfoot those with bars of silver. Scatter the peoples who take pleasure in war" (Ps 68:30). They prayed and praised God that "there he shatters the bow's flaming arrows, the shield, the sword, and the weapons of war. You are resplendent and majestic coming down from the mountains of prey. The brave-hearted have been plundered; they have slipped into their final sleep. None of the warriors was able to lift a hand" (Ps 76:3–5). War is associated with the evildoers and adversaries who afflict God's people, from whom God delivers and saves: "When evildoers came against me to devour my flesh, my foes and my enemies stumbled and fell. Though an army deploys against me, my heart will not be afraid; though a war breaks out against me, I will still be confident" (Ps 27:2–3).

Some Christians might believe that these passages are best understood by spiritualizing them, taking them to refer to spiritual war against the enemies of the world, the flesh, and the devil because, ultimately, "our struggle is not against flesh and blood, but against the rulers, against the authorities, against the cosmic powers of this darkness, against evil, spiritual forces in the heavens" (Eph 6:12). While that is a defensible interpretation in light of the New Testament, that does not replace or obviate the plain, literal meaning of the text as referring to physical violence from human enemies who want to hurt or kill us. Many Christians in the developed world enjoy relative freedom from that kind of enmity, because of which some may be uncomfortable with the literal meaning of these passages referring to other people as enemies. Theirs is a rare experience; most people in most places throughout most of history would easily understand that, sometimes, other people wish us harm, and these psalms would give them great comfort. God commands us to love our enemies, not to pretend we do not have any.

God Is a Warrior Who Fights for His People

Despite the overwhelmingly negative portrayal of war in most of the Bible, there is another aspect to it. War teaches us something about God's character. God promises to fight for his people (Exod 14:14; Deut 1:30; 20:4; Josh 10:25; Isa 31:4–5; Zech 14:3). In Exodus 15, after Israel is delivered through the Red Sea from Pharaoh's pursuing army, Moses sings:

> I will sing to the LORD,
> for he is highly exalted;
> he has thrown the horse
> and its rider into the sea.
> The LORD is my strength and my song;
> he has become my salvation.
> This is my God, and I will praise him,
> my father's God, and I will exalt him. The LORD is a warrior;
> the LORD is his name. (vv. 1–3)

Moses was not speaking metaphorically. God had just gone to war and wiped out Pharoah's army more completely than any human army could. Later, Isaiah echoes the same praise: "The LORD advances like a warrior; he stirs up his zeal like a soldier. He shouts, he roars aloud, he prevails over his enemies" (Isa 42:13). King David is called a "man of war" (1 Sam 16:18 KJV), and he gives thanks that God "trains my hands for war; my arms can bend a bow of bronze" (2 Sam 22:35; Ps 18:34). Again, David was not being metaphorical. His first notable act in the Bible is to kill Goliath. He led troops in battle and, on one occasion, killed two hundred Philistines and presented their foreskins to King Saul as dowry to marry his daughter (1 Samuel 18). David sings of God's blessings on his war-making prowess in Messianic passages that describe the future Anointed King's triumph and reign (2 Sam 22:35 and Ps 18:34; see also Ps 144:1). God wages war against his enemies and the enemies of his people—always spiritually but sometimes physically as well.

There are three implications of the God being a "man of war." First, as I mentioned earlier, that God is a "man of war" is a way of showing that war is not wholly evil and that the Bible does not require pacifism. Second, we can learn about the character of God by reflecting on, or even participating in, war. I suggest that the image of God as a warrior teaches us that God is active and engaged on behalf of his people; that he consciously opposes those who would harm them; that he is *armed*, so to speak, with power and might to accomplish his will; that he is focused, determined, and purposeful (warriors are trained and disciplined, not amateurs); that he "stirs up his zeal" and fights hard; that he is following a plan (warriors are strategic, not random); and that those whom he opposes deserve his wrath. We can gain a deeper understanding of these aspects of God's character by understanding war. Just as the verse "our God is a consuming fire" (Heb 12:29) is more intelligible and frightening if you have ever put your hand on a hot stove or witnessed a building consumed in flames, in the same way we might gain a visceral, experiential appreciation of aspects of God's character by serving in the military in a just war.

Incidentally, this sheds light on the New Testament passages that use military metaphors to describe the spiritual life, as when Paul speaks of another law "waging war against the law of my mind" (Rom 7:23) and urges us to "fight the good fight" (1 Tim 6:12) and "put on the full armor of God" (Eph 6:11); as when James warns against "passions that wage war within you" (Jas 4:1); and as when Peter warns against the "sinful desires that wage war against the soul" (1 Pet 2:11). We are, all of us, combatants in a war for our souls. We are to emulate God and be men and women of war in our zeal, discipline, power, and purposefulness in waging war against sin, the flesh, and the devil.

Third, and more to the point of this book, we can learn something about the character of a just war. If we can learn about God through war, we can also learn about war through God. If our wars are to be at all justifiable, they must, as far as possible—and within the bounds of the state's institutional authority—reflect the character of God. This requires a fine distinction. God fights for a *specific purpose*—to defend his people and glorify his name—that is not within the purview of the secular state. Governments should not wage war for a sectarian purpose. But God also fights from, and for, his *general sovereignty*—to defend, vindicate, and restore his rule—that lays down the template for earthly governments. (I expand on this in the next chapter.) In that sense, the purpose, execution, and outcome of earthly war should be *righteous*: it should be characterized by justice, a concern for peace, and a respect for human dignity and human flourishing. How to do that with the blunt and bloody instrument of war is a difficult question—to which the just war tradition is the answer.

War Is an Image of Final Judgment

The final judgment, the day of the Lord, the apocalypse at the end of history is presented as a culminating battle, a final war to end all wars. Daniel 7–12 records a series of wars that seem to prefigure the final judgment, echoed in Revelation 11–13 and 16–17 (including the famed battle of Armageddon). Joel 2 envisions "a great and strong people" (v. 2) who swarm the earth in judgment such that "the earth quakes before them; the sky shakes. The sun and moon grow dark, and the stars cease their shining" (v. 10). The swarm is God's army come to bring judgment: "The Lord makes his voice heard in the presence of his army. His camp is very large; those who carry out his command are powerful. Indeed, the day of the Lord is terrible and dreadful—who can endure it?" (v. 11). In fact, it will be the people of redeemed Israel who are God's weapon against the rebellious nations. God says to his people:

> You are my war club,
> my weapons of war.
> With you I will smash nations;
> with you I will bring kingdoms to ruin.
> With you I will smash the horse and its rider;
> with you I will smash the chariot and its rider.
> With you I will smash man and woman;
> with you I will smash the old man and the youth;
> with you I will smash the young man and the young woman.
> With you I will smash the shepherd and his flock;
> with you I will smash the farmer and his ox-team.
> With you I will smash governors and officials. (Jer 51:20–23)

These images come together in one of the most breathtaking passages of Scripture: the image of King Jesus astride a white horse in command of the armies of heaven to wage a final war against the nations and against the beast in whose thrall they rebel against God's rightful reign. We see this image of Jesus in Revelation 19 where "with justice he judges and makes war" (v. 11). Behind him, "the armies that were in heaven followed him on white horses, wearing pure white linen" (v. 14). Against them on the field of battle, "I saw the beast, the kings of the earth, and their armies gathered together to wage war against the rider on the horse and against his army" (v. 19). The beast and his false prophet are "thrown alive into the lake of fire that burns with sulfur" (v. 20) while "the rest were killed with the sword that came from the mouth of the rider on the horse, and all the birds ate their fill of their flesh" (v. 21). War is an act of judgment. God, the perfect judge, will bring his enemies to a final end through a final battle that will judge his enemies and vindicate his reign and his people once and for all. This is the one and only perfectly just war because it will usher in unblemished justice for eternity.

We should take two lessons from this. First, although men throughout history have repeatedly proclaimed their wars to be the last battle and the final vindication of justice, history continues to march on. No war on earth is ever perfectly just, and none will end war forever. H. G. Wells, a British progressive, called World War I "the war to end war,"[22] and he was quickly proven wrong. There is no "war to end all war" this side of heaven because King Jesus is the only one who is worthy to wage that battle. That may be one reason God forbade King David from building the temple: he wanted to remind David (and us) that though David prefigured the Messiah in being a "man of war," David was, nonetheless, sinful and his wars inevitably tarnished with sin. God wanted to spare his people the temptation of seeing David as the full realization of the perfect judge and king or mistaking his wars as the final conquest of sin, death, and hell.

Second, despite our sin, our wars are acts of judgment. If our wars are to be just and to reflect the character of God, they must reflect, insofar as possible, the image of the one truly just war we find in Scripture. Our wars are inevitably acts of judgment against those whom we fight, and we are accountable to God to judge justly. Again, Paul reminds us that the ruler "does not carry the sword for no reason. For it is God's servant, an avenger that brings wrath on the one who does wrong" (Rom 13:4). To wield the sword on earth against wrongdoers is to judge, convict, and to carry out a sentence on them, which again reminds us that war must only be fought for and with justice. We feel intuitively that the war against

---

[22] H. G. Wells, *In the Fourth Year* (Copenhagen: Saga Egmont, 1918, 2022); he called it "the war to end *all* war" just four years earlier, in his book *The War That Will End War* (London: Frank & Cecil Palmer, 1914); emphasis added.

the Nazis was right simply because they deserved judgment. All just wars should, in principle, be an exercise of righteous judgment.

God Will End War

God's war to end all war ends in victory. God wins, and war ends. God promises his people that "you shall look for those who contend with you, but you will not find them. Those who war against you will become absolutely nothing" (Isa 41:12). Through the prophet Zechariah, God says, "I will cut off the chariot from Ephraim and the horse from Jerusalem. The bow of war will be removed, and he will proclaim peace to the nations. His dominion will extend from sea to sea, from the Euphrates River to the ends of the earth" (Zech 9:9–10). And through Hosea: "On that day I will make a covenant for them with the wild animals, the birds of the sky, and the creatures that crawl on the ground. I will shatter bow, sword, and weapons of war in the land and will enable the people to rest securely" (Hos 2:18). Most famously:

> In the last days
> the mountain of the LORD's house will be established
> at the top of the mountains
> and will be raised above the hills.
> All nations will stream to it,
> and many peoples will come and say,
> "Come, let's go up to the mountain of the LORD,
> to the house of the God of Jacob.
> He will teach us about his ways
> so that we may walk in his paths."
> For instruction will go out of Zion
> and the word of the LORD from Jerusalem.

> He will settle disputes among the nations
> and provide arbitration for many peoples.
> They will beat their swords into plows
> and their spears into pruning knives.
> Nation will not take up the sword against nation,
> and they will never again train for war. (Isa 2:2–4; see also
> Mic 4:3)

Conclusion

The Bible does not command pacifism or condone holy war or realism. The Bible reflects the reality that war is almost always terrible and that it is right to plead for God to spare us from its evils. But the Bible also shows another side to war: that God is a man of war. That means we can learn about him through reflection on war—and learn about war through reflection on him. What we learn about war is that, just as God uses war as an act of judgment, so too we should aspire for our wars to carefully reflect God's judgment and God's justice in how, who, and why we fight. That does not mean we are to fight holy wars in God's name, which is not within the jurisdiction of earthly governments. Rather, it means that just as earthly governments must govern justly, so too must they war justly—that is, they must fight war to accomplish justice, and for no other reason.

This raises the next question. What, biblically speaking, is justice?

2

Sovereignty, Justice, and Natural Law in the Bible

War must be fought for the sake of "justice." That invites a rather large, important, and obvious question: What is justice? The question is as old as human civilization. Philosophers and theologians have sought the answer for millennia. The question is also central to the Christian life. When summarizing man's duty to God, the prophet Micah wrote, "What does the LORD require of you but to do justice, and to love kindness, and to walk humbly with your God?" (Mic 6:8 ESV). Understanding justice is one step in understanding the character of our God and how to honor him with our lives. What does it mean to "do justice"?

We intuitively understand that to do justice is to do the right thing, to be fair to others, to give them their due, perhaps also to be lawful. But that intuitive definition is vague. What is "the right thing"? What are others due? What is fairness? What is the standard of merit? How do we determine what is owed? If it is good to be just but justice is whatever is upright or good, we have backed ourselves into a definitional cul-de-sac, a tautology where justice and goodness point to each other with no other referent.

It helps to understand what realm of activity we are discussing when we talk about justice. Justice is the virtue of political excellence, the *telos* of political activity—though I mean "political" in a different way than many readers may assume.[1] I do not mean, primarily, elections, polls, voting, and the ups and downs of political parties. *Politics* is deeper and broader than that. Politics is about how a group of people is ordered; how their relationships are arranged; whether and how people receive their due; how rulers become rulers; how rulers use power and to what ends; and how rulers make decisions. One political scientist defined politics as "who gets what, when, how," which perfectly reflects twentieth-century assumptions about the nature of government.[2] Politics is about the contest for, and use of, power. To "do justice" is to get and use power rightly.

If we are doing politics well, we are doing justice. To ask, "What is justice?" is the same as asking, "What is politics for?" What is the rightful goal toward which political activity should aim? What should be our governing principle, our ordering framework, our standards of right and wrong when we engage in politics? We use the word *justice* to name that governing principle, but we still need to ask what it looks like in action. What does the Bible say about politics? About the purpose of government? This chapter is a primer on political theology, or the doctrine of civil government. I review basic concepts, including sovereignty, justice, natural law, and the separation

---

[1] Borrowing from Aristotle the notion that virtue is a characteristic of excellence for a given activity.

[2] See Harold D. Lasswell, *Politics: Who Gets What, When, How* (Tauranga, NZ: Papamoa, 2018).

of church and state. There are entire shelves devoted to these issues. My goal is to present a summary to show how these ideas relate and how they form an integrated biblical theology of government, with specific attention to the government's mandate to wield the sword.

God's Kingship

To say that the Bible has a lot to say about justice and politics is an understatement. From one perspective, when we broaden our understanding of *politics*, we see that justice and rulership are perhaps the main themes of the entire Bible because the Bible is the story of God's kingship. "I am the Lord, your Holy One, the Creator of Israel, your King," God proclaims through the prophet Isaiah (Isa 43:15; see also Isa 6:5; 33:17; 33:22; 44:6, and Zeph 3:15). God is king because he is creator. We, his vice-regents, exercise dominion on his behalf over the earth. He exercises his kingship through covenant love of his people. His covenant is a sort of constitution of his kingdom (though the modern connotation of "constitution" is too impersonal and legalistic to capture the full meaning of "covenant"). Those who reject his kingship are in rebellion against him; sin is sedition against the rightful ruler of the universe.

How does God wield his sovereignty? The Bible repeatedly shows that God will defend his people, vindicate his kingship, punish and defeat his enemies, and reestablish his rule against rebellion. He does so through the intercession of his Anointed One, revealed to be Jesus Christ, the King of kings, of whom Isaiah prophesied that "the government will be on his shoulders" (Isa 9:6). Jesus's incarnation inaugurates the kingdom of God, and his return will consummate his rule. The core of Jesus's message, the first announcement of his gospel, is that "the kingdom of God has come near" (Mark 1:15). The Bible's storyline culminates at the end of history when "the kingdom of the world has become the kingdom of our Lord and of his Christ, and he will reign forever and ever" (Rev 11:15).

Note how thoroughly political the Bible's storyline is, in the sense that it is concerned with rulership, sovereignty, and power.[3] The psalmists remind us that "the LORD loves justice" (Ps 37:28; 33:5) and that "righteousness and justice are the foundation of [his] throne" (89:14). God's kingship is the model or template of sovereignty; it provides a concrete example and definition of what sovereignty is for. His is the original and only infallible government, of which earthly governments are a pale reflection. God's kingship tells us what politics is for.

Earthly governments, when they govern well, are images of God's rulership: to govern justly means, in a sense, to govern like God. The Bible clearly expects rulers to rule justly, and it condemns oppression. Take just a selection of Proverbs: "It is by me [wisdom] that kings reign and rulers enact just law; by me, princes lead, as do nobles and all righteous judges" (Prov 8:15–16) and "Wicked behavior is detestable to kings, since a throne is established by righteousness" (16:12), echoing the language of Psalm 89 that righteousness is the foundation of God's throne. Finally, "A wicked ruler over a helpless people is like a roaring lion or a charging bear. A leader who lacks understanding is very oppressive, but one who hates dishonest profit prolongs his life" (Prov 28:15–16).

Like God's rulership of his people, just government is not oppressive but seeks the good of the governed. The Bible is clear that, when done well, the exercise of power can be a great blessing. King David, with his dying benediction, shared his insight that "the

---

[3] For a full biblical theology of God's kingship, see Thomas R. Schreiner, *The King in His Beauty: A Biblical Theology of the Old and New Testaments* (Grand Rapids: Baker, 2013).

one who rules the people with justice, who rules in the fear of God, is like the morning light when the sun rises on a cloudless morning, the glisten of rain on sprouting grass" (2 Sam 23:3–4). Just government results in the flourishing of the governed.

What can we learn from God's kingship that is applicable to earthly government? What is the *telos* of political rule, the purpose of sovereignty? Like God, just rulers wield legitimate authority to judge rightly between right and wrong. Just rulers defend themselves, their rule, their people, and their realm. Just rulers punish rebels and uphold order. Just rulers govern under the terms of a covenant, or a covenant-like arrangement that describes the relationship between ruler and ruled and outlines the jurisdiction of the rulers' powers. Above all, just rulers love their people and work for their good and their flourishing. To rule this way is to *do justice.*

Israel: *Mishpat* and *Tzadeqah*

Does the Bible give us a picture of what just governance looks like in practice? Throughout history, many eager philosophers, politicians, and theologians have searched the Bible for a model of the ideal regime and a picture of justice in action. They encounter the Israel of the Old Testament, and quite often, they pull from it whatever fits their preconceived political agenda.

One can find arguments that Israel is a model of (1) socialism because farmers were to leave the gleanings of their fields for the poor (Lev 19:9–10) and periodically forgive all debts, wiping the slate clean with the Year of Jubilee (Leviticus 25). Or Israel is a model of (2) nationalism because the people were to keep themselves separate and distinct from the surrounding nations (Lev 18:3); or of (3) capitalism because Israel had private property, forbade theft, engaged in trade, and used currency; or of (4) slavery because Israel permitted legalized slavery. Perhaps Israel is a model of (5) constitutional monarchy because it had a divinely anointed king with delimited powers—or of (6) the opposite, tyranny, because the prophet Samuel warned against the inevitable abuses of monarchy (1 Samuel 8). Israel might be a model of (7) libertarian independence where every peasant farmer shall "sit under his grapevine and under his fig tree" (Mic 4:4). Maybe Israel is a model of (8) holy war because of its God-ordained wars of genocide against Canaan; or maybe Israel is a model of (9) pacifism, in which the people of God shall "beat their swords into plows" (Mic 4:3).

The first thing to say about biblical Israel is that being a model for contemporary secular politics is not the main point of biblical Israel. God formed the people of Israel, made them his people, and made a covenant with them to reveal his character and unfold his plan of redemption. Israel existed to prepare the way for the Messiah. Whatever we may glean from Israel about how governments might govern justly is peripheral to Israel's main purpose. We must keep that in mind to avoid doing violence to the text. Debates about socialism versus capitalism were foreign to the ancient world and would have been meaningless to the original audience; we should be extremely cautious about retrospectively reading our debates into Israel's experience.

With that caution in mind, we can, perhaps, look for examples of wisdom and prudence in Israel's history. Israel was to be a "light for the nations" (Isa 49:6)—primarily by being the vehicle through which the Messiah comes but also, in a lesser sense, by being an ethical model of what justice and righteousness looked like in practice. Again, the prophets clearly applied the moral law to other nations, condemning Babylon, Assyria, and Persia for oppression, tyranny, and violence. The moral law God specifically revealed to Israel did not apply only to Israel; it applies to all people, everywhere, at all times, and Israel was to be a living embodiment or model of what it looked like to live that moral law out together. Theologians have often looked to the second tablet of the Ten Commandments—the prohibitions against murder, adultery, theft, deceit, and envy—as the first expressions of a universal natural law.[4] In other words, when God instructs Israel about justice and righteousness, he is instructing all of us. The moral laws and the general principles of justice we find in God's commands to Israel do not apply only to Israel. It is to these general principles we should look when we look to Israel as a political model.[5]

We see the principles of justice in Israel's life through the Old Testament's repeated use of two related words, *mishpat* and *tzadeqah*, usually translated "justice" and "righteousness," respectively. The Old Testament regularly pairs these two words and sometimes uses them interchangeably, suggesting a very close relationship between them. *Mishpat* means to treat people equitably, to give them their rights or their due, to show no partiality in judgment, to render a just decision in a court case. It includes what we might call procedural justice (following legal rules to ensure fairness and consistency) and rectifying justice (punishing wrongdoers and giving restitution to victims).

Tzadeqah focuses on right relationships, first with God and then with everyone else. It is the justice of a rightly ordered whole, the justice of a flourishing society, of a person's character and habits. It

---

[4] For a fuller discussion of natural law, see another volume in this series, David VanDrunen, *Natural Law: A Short Companion* (Brentwood, TN: B&H Academic, 2023). See also Andrew T. Walker, *Faithful Reason: Natural Law Ethics for God's Glory and Our Good* (Brentwood, TN: B&H Academic, 2024).

[5] That does not mean the civil and ceremonial laws apply directly to us today. Few argue that we are called to emulate Israel's theocracy or institute a complex system of temple worship, animal sacrifice, and ritual cleanliness. How exactly we draw the lines and distinguish among Israel's many laws is a complex and debated topic, mostly beyond the scope of this volume.

includes what we might call substantive justice or primary justice, the justice of equal opportunity and of respecting the intrinsic dignity of all. It is the characteristic or trait of a rightly ordered person or society.[6] *Mishpat* is closer to the kind of justice we often hear about from politically conservative groups, concerned with legal fairness and individual rights, while *tzadeqah* is closer to what we often hear about from politically progressive groups, concerned with equality and recognition. The two should, ideally, go together: doing *mishpat* helps restore *tzadeqah* when it has been violated by wrongdoers. As Bruce K. Waltke and Ivan D. V. De Silva explain, "If righteousness establishes right order, *justice* (*mispat*) restores the violated order by delivering the victim and punishing the offender to produce shalom."[7]

The subtle difference between *mishpat* and *tzadeqah* echoes a contemporary debate about the nature of justice. Is justice mainly concerned with the right ordering of the whole of society (which seems to correspond with *tzadeqah*) or with individual rights (loosely akin to *mishpat*)? Is justice about right, or rights? The distinction is, at least partly, illusory. It is hard to have individual rights in a society that is not rightly ordered, and a right ordering of society *without* individual rights seems to be nonsensical. The right ordering of society is a precondition for individual rights to mean anything—while the protection of individual rights is an important part of the right ordering of society, especially at the ground level from the perspective of an individual citizen. That is likely one

---

[6] See Timothy Keller, *Generous Justice: How God's Grace Makes Us Just* (New York: Penguin, 2012); see William L. Holladay, ed., *A Concise Hebrew and Aramaic Lexicon of the Old Testament* (Grand Rapids: Eerdmans, 1971), 221, 303.

[7] Bruce K. Waltke and Ivan D. V. De Silva, *Proverbs: A Shorter Commentary* (Grand Rapids: Eerdmans, 2021), 37. Many thanks to David Fullerton for help with Hebrew.

reason the Bible pairs *mishpat* and *tzadeqah* together so frequently and so tightly.[8] Waltke and De Silva clarify, "Justice is more than legal action; it is a moral quality, coming from the heart. To live rightly is to do justice and righteousness."[9]

Israel was commanded to place special emphasis on *mishpat* for the powerless. A *mishpat* society is one that pays attention to giving *mishpat* to the poor. Moses tells the people, "You must not deny justice to a poor person among you in his lawsuit" (Exod 23:6) and "the one who denies justice to the resident alien, a fatherless child, or a widow is cursed" (Deut 27:19; see also Deut 10:17–19). The prophets echo the emphasis on justice for the poor: "This is what the Lord says: Administer justice and righteousness. Rescue the victim of robbery from his oppressor. Don't exploit or brutalize the resident alien, the fatherless, or the widow. Don't shed innocent blood in this place" (Jer 22:3).

Mishpat and *tzadeqah* often occur together and present a picture of wholistic, just society. Consider two passages:

> Happy is the one whose help is the God of Jacob, whose hope is in the Lord his God, the Maker of heaven and

---

[8] See Jonathan Leeman, *Political Church: The Local Assembly as Embassy of Christ's Rule* (Downers Grove, IL: InterVarsity, 2016); Nicholas Wolterstorff, *Justice: Rights and Wrongs* (Princeton, NJ: Princeton Univ. Press, 2008); David VanDrunen, *Politics after Christendom: Political Theology in a Fractured World* (Grand Rapids: Zondervan, 2020), chaps. 9 and 11. While I broadly agree with Van Drunen's conclusion that the government should pursue "protectionist" goals and that "perfectionist" aims are an "uncomfortable fit" with the Noahic covenant, I suggest that the pursuit of *tzadeqah* may oblige us to invite that discomfort in some cases. Put another way, *tzadeqah* is a reminder that any justice worth the name should properly strive for more than mere rectifying and procedural justice, even when it is uncomfortable.

[9] Waltke and de Silva, *Proverbs*, 37.

> earth, the sea and everything in them. He remains faithful forever, executing justice for the exploited and giving food to the hungry. The LORD frees prisoners. The LORD opens the eyes of the blind. The LORD raises up those who are oppressed. The LORD loves the righteous. The LORD protects resident aliens and helps the fatherless and the widow, but he frustrates the ways of the wicked. (Ps 146:5–9)

> When they heard me, they blessed me, and when they saw me, they spoke well of me. For I rescued the poor who cried out for help, and the fatherless child who had no one to support him. The dying blessed me, and I made the widow's heart rejoice. I clothed myself in righteousness, and it enveloped me; my just decisions were like a robe and a turban. I was eyes to the blind and feet to the lame. I was a father to the needy, and I examined the case of the stranger. I shattered the fangs of the unjust and snatched the prey from his teeth. (Job 29:11–17)

These two passages offer a detailed and concrete picture of what was expected of Israel, what it would have looked like to do justice and righteousness. It means to be attentive to the needs of the oppressed, the hungry, the prisoners, the bowed down, the poor, the fatherless, and the widow.

Does this mean that government should always favor the poor? Do the rich and powerful not have rights? Taken in isolation, some of these verses seem to imply that the ruler should be a class warrior, always taking the side of the poor against the rich. If so, we have nothing to lose but our chains, and all Christians should be communists. This is why it is important always to interpret Scripture in light of the whole of Scripture. In Exodus 23, Moses does indeed command, "You must not deny justice to a poor person among you in his lawsuit" (v. 6), but only after saying a few verses earlier, "Do not show favoritism to a poor person in his lawsuit" (v. 3). Moses insists on impartiality, not favoritism for the poor.

So why the emphasis, in the rest of Scripture, on being attentive to the poor? Because they are the ones who need defending. The rich and powerful can often take care of themselves and are rarely the victims of judicial bias. The Bible is realistic about how fallen human societies work, and history bears out the Bible's vision. The rich and powerful usually call the shots, and if the shots are unfair, it is the poor and disenfranchised who suffer. A ruler who wants to rule justly will govern with an awareness of the vulnerability of the poor and be especially attentive to their needs. (Historically, there is an exception. During periods of revolution, especially populist or communist revolutions, the rich are often scapegoated as the criminals behind all social evils. They are targeted for mob violence and their property stolen in mass expropriation or nationalization schemes—none of which the Bible condones.)

To jump ahead a few thousand years, this helps explain what might otherwise seem an oddity in Thomas Aquinas's understanding of justice. In Aquinas's magisterial *Summa Theologica*, he quotes the conventional definition of justice—to render to each his due—but includes liberality or charity in his discussion: "Mercy, liberality, and the like, are connected with [justice] . . . To succor the needy, which belongs to mercy or pity, and to be liberally beneficent, which pertains to liberality, are by a kind of reduction ascribed to justice as to their principal virtue."[10] Aquinas

[10] ST II-II, Q58, Article 12, in Thomas Aquinas, *On Law, Morality, and Politics*, ed. William P. Baumgarth and Richard J. Regan (Indianapolis: Hackett, 1988), 162.

seems to be arguing that justice entails and requires generosity and charity. His claim is counterintuitive because justice is giving to each their due while charity is giving beyond what one is legally required to give. How does Aquinas square the circle? He seems to mean that human beings possess intrinsic dignity and worth because they are made in the image of God, that no one deserves the indignity of poverty or suffering, and that to give the needy succor is to recognize their worth and treat them with the dignity they deserve—not the desert of their legal rights but the desert of their inherent moral worth.

Christian philosopher Nicholas Wolterstorff argues that the Bible supports the idea of inherent natural rights—even for the poor. God merits worship and is entitled to our obedience. To give God his due—to do justice to him—is to recognize his right to be worshiped and to be obeyed. But human beings are made in God's image. We, too, merit something: not worship, but certainly some degree of recognition, respect, and honor. We, too, have an inherent natural right to receive our due. Wolterstorff maintains, "Once one has said that God has worth, that that worth grounds God's right to worship and obedience, and that human beings likewise have worth, it proves impossible not to continue in this line of thought and hold that human beings have rights on account of their worth."[11] That this applies especially to the downtrodden is a unique emphasis of the Bible's vision of justice. "God desires that each and every human being shall flourish, that each and every shall experience what the Old Testament writers call shalom," Wolterstorff argues, "God desires the flourishing of each and every one of God's human creatures; justice is

[11] Nicholas Wolterstorff, *Justice: Rights and Wrongs* (Princeton, NJ: Princeton Univ. Press, 2008), 95.

indispensable to that. Love and justice are not pitted against each other but intertwined."[12]

Romans 13: Order, Peace, and Justice

So far, we have seen that God's kingship defines sovereignty, that sovereigns should govern for the good of their people, that Old Testament Israel is an indirect model of what that looks like, and that the Old Testament *mishpat* and *tzadeqah* give us pictures of justice in action. The New Testament furthers and reinforces these principles. Let us look again at Paul's letter to the Romans.

To set the stage, recall it was Pontius Pilate, a Roman governor, who ordered Jesus's execution, and the Roman Empire occupied Israel and carved up its territory into Roman provinces. Rome was tolerant of all kinds of paganism but hostile to the monotheist Jews and the new Christian sect. In the decades following Jesus's death, Rome would become more explicitly pagan and theocratic. Though Paul was a Roman citizen, as far as the Roman authorities were concerned Paul was a member of a despised minority sect that refused to participate in Rome's pagan traditions. Refusal to participate also meant that Paul was cut off from much of civic life—that is why the Romans looked at the Jews and Christians as suspect and possibly traitorous. To refuse to worship Rome's gods could be seen as a kind of sedition. Just a few years after this letter, Paul was arrested and eventually executed by Rome.

In that context, Paul could hardly write a manifesto lecturing Rome on the duties of government or telling Caesar how to do his job. About a century before Paul, the famous Roman senator Marcus Cicero had openly opposed the Roman Empire for

[12] Wolterstorff, *Justice*, 82.

destroying traditional republican liberty—and he was assassinated for his trouble. There was no freedom of speech or press; Paul had to be careful what he wrote. If Paul was too bold or offensive—if he called for revolution or challenged the legitimacy of the empire—he could get not only himself killed but also incite empire-wide persecution against all Jews and Christians. Paul had to step carefully.

Nonetheless, he did manage to describe what government should—and should not—do, outlining a charter for government and charging it to keep peace, order, and justice. Rulers "bear the sword" to bring terror to bad conduct and to bring God's wrath on the wrongdoer. Paul is building on the Noahic covenant of Genesis 9. In Genesis 9, after the flood, God tells Noah "Whoever sheds human blood, by humans his blood will be shed, for God made humans in his image" (Gen 9:6). God specifically says "by humans" shall the murderer's blood be shed. God delegates to us, to human beings, the authority and responsibility for keeping violent disorder in check.[13] Here in Romans 13, Paul similarly uses a violent image, that of rulers who "carry the sword." That was not a metaphor; he was being literal. Armed soldiers bearing swords patrolled cities, arrested and executed criminals, put down rebellions, and otherwise enforced order. And Paul reminds us that government does this "for your good" (v. 4).

Order is good. We often worry, rightly, about government having too much power, and we will talk about that shortly—but in a sense, that is a First World problem. In some parts of the world, governments do not have enough power—and in a few places, there essentially is no government at all. In those cases, the richest

---

[13] David VanDrunen has persuasively argued that Romans 13 is building on the Noahic covenant of Genesis 9 and that the Noahic covenant is the primary authorizing text for civil government in the Bible. See VanDrunen, *Politics after Christendom*, chaps. 3–4.

or best-armed warlord does whatever he wants—which usually includes fighting others in a competition for power and abusing the powerless. The alternative to government is not utopian freedom, but anarchy. There is no Christian case for anarchism. Governments that fail to enforce order are failing at the first and most basic duty of government.

Paul does not stop at his exhortation to keep order. Rulers should also pursue justice. We see the call for justice in four places, each of which gives us a perspective on what doing justice involves. First, in v. 2 we read that those who resist will incur "judgment." The word could also be translated "verdict" or even "lawsuit." It is like saying that if you resist government, you will be sued, or you will be given a sentence by a judge. These are legal terms. Paul, of course, means that God is the ultimate judge, but it is clear from the passage that the ruler is also a judge, one who distinguishes between right and wrong, just and unjust, and passes sentences accordingly. Earthly government has the responsibility to discern what is just, and it has rightful authority to act on that discernment.

Second, rulers should be a terror to bad conduct, not good conduct (v. 3). That means, again, that rulers should distinguish between the two rather than rule arbitrarily. This is both a responsibility (judge rightly) but also a limitation: rulers do not get to do whatever they want. There is a standard of right and wrong that stands outside and above the rulers that defines what rulers are supposed to do. They are accountable to an objective, timeless, external standard outside and above themselves. They are accountable to God, who gave them authority, for using their authority rightly. Jesus is still King; he gives Caesar earthly authority for the ministry of justice and order, and Jesus, not Caesar, defines what is just. Jesus told Pilate, "You would have no authority over me at all if it hadn't been given you from above" (John 19:11).

Third, Paul describes the government as God's avenger to punish wrongdoing (Rom 13:4). Interestingly, the original Greek for "avenger," *ekdikos*, means "costumed superhero in a shared fictional universe." (Just kidding.) In fact, the "avenger" mentioned here is almost the opposite of Marvel's Avengers. The caped crusaders of the movies are usually vigilantes, acting outside the law and without authorization. (The entire plot of *Captain America: Civil War* revolved around an effort to regulate and legalize the Avengers by bringing them under legitimate authority.) When Paul calls the earthly rulers God's avenger, he is saying they do in fact have God's authority to execute justice. The Greek for "avenger" (seriously this time) means "public advocate," "prosecutor," or "legal representative," one who pursues justice on behalf of another.[14] Government stands in God's stead as his advocate and representative for the purpose of earthly justice and order.

To get the full flavor of this, we need to go back to Romans 12. Paul writes there: "Friends, do not avenge yourselves; instead leave room for God's wrath, because it is written, 'Vengeance belongs to me; I will repay, says the Lord'" (v. 19). The word for "avenger" shares the same root with "vengeance." In chapter 12, Paul is speaking to individuals, and he tells them not to avenge themselves because God will do it for them. Then in the next chapter, he says that government is the avenger. God will take vengeance, and he has delegated it to government to be the earthly executor of that task. (See also 1 Thess 4:6—"the Lord is an avenger.")

Fourth, Paul tells us, "Pay your obligations to everyone" (Rom 13:7). While he is addressing the reader and, by extension, the

---

[14] See Henry George Liddell and Robert Scott, *Greek-English Lexicon*, 9th ed. (New York: Oxford Univ. Press, 1996), s.v. εκδῐκ-εω; accessed online at https://lsj.gr/wiki/Main_Page.

common citizen, he is also affirming the conventional definition of justice widespread in the ancient world. Cicero defined justice as "the virtue which assigns to each his due,"[15] and the emperor Justinian opened his famous *Institutes* by proclaiming that "justice is the set and constant purpose which gives to every man his due,"[16] which is the definition that Thomas Aquinas would pick up and quote in his *Summa Theologica* as the definition of justice. Coming on the heels of all the other reminders Paul gives in the passage about the role of government in upholding justice, this seems another subtle way of underlining the point: rulers should give to all what they are due.

In all four places in Romans 13, we see that rulers wield legitimate authority, but their authority is neither boundless nor self-justifying. They are given a specific charge—uphold justice and order—and the definition of "justice" comes from outside. They do not get to make up what counts as "justice." The government's authority is not a plenary grant of discretionary power that the ruler may use in any way for whatever purpose. Government is accountable to God to do what governments are supposed to do. King Jesus has defined the charter for earthly rulers; he has given them a specific and limited charge. Just as there is no Christian case for anarchy, there is also no case for unfettered rule, for tyranny or totalitarianism.

Paul's argument here is crucial because rulers throughout history have resisted it. One example is close to home: President Richard Nixon was forced to resign after inconvertible evidence surfaced of his criminal conduct. After he left office, Nixon tried to

---

[15] Marcusi Tullius Cicero, *De Natura Deorum (On the Nature of the Gods)* trans. Francis Brooks (London: Methuen, 1896), 3:XV. Available online at https://oll.libertyfund.org/titles/cicero-on-the-nature-of-the-gods.

[16] For Justinian's *Institutes*, see https://gutenberg.org/cache/epub/5983/pg5983-images.html.

justify his behavior. "When the president does it, that means it is not illegal," he claimed.[17] In his view, presidents are, by definition, incapable of committing a crime when they claim their action is in defense of national security. Nixon's claim calls to mind Louis XIV, the absolutist king of France in the seventeenth century, who supposedly claimed, "*L'Etat, c'est moi*" ("The State, it's me," or "I am the State"), a claim so famously villainous that George Lucas put a version of it into the mouth of Emperor Palpatine in *Star Wars* ("I *am* the Senate!"). Nixon, Louis, and Palpatine believed that the king was the law, such that whatever the king did was legal by virtue of the king being the one who did it.[18]

The Bible directly undermines such claims. We should expect our government, even in a sinful and fallen world, to uphold order and strive for justice. If it does not, it is failing to be a government. The duty of government to govern justly is so important it seems to be the defining trait of what makes a government a government. Augustine famously asked, "Justice removed, then, what are kingdoms but great bands of robbers?"[19] If a government systemically flouts or ignores justice, deliberately and persistently rules unjustly on purpose as a matter of policy—a government that is totalitarian or genocidal—it is not a government; it is a criminal conspiracy pretending to be a government.

The ruler is not supposed to uphold mere order, or brute order, or order at all costs—the order of tyranny and oppression.

---

[17] "Transcript of David Frost's Interview with Richard Nixon," 1977. https://teachingamericanhistory.org/document/transcript-of-david-frosts-interview-with-richard-nixon/.

[18] See Herbert H. Rowen, "'L'Etat c'est Moi': Louis XIV and the State."

[19] Augustine, *The City of God Against the Pagans*, ed. R. W. Dyson (Cambridge: Cambridge Univ. Press, 1998), 147.

It should be a just order. The Roman historian Tacitus famously criticized the empire for its brutality; after one campaign in which the Romans wiped out whole cities, he said Rome would "make a desert, and call it peace."[20] A desert is peaceful because it is lifeless. That is not the order the Bible calls for. It calls for a life-sustaining just peace that fosters the good of the whole society and all the people in it. Augustine argued in the fifth century that "in comparison with the peace of the just, the peace of the unjust is not worthy to be called peace at all."[21] True justice and true peace go together.

Natural Law

To do justice, rulers must discern between right and wrong. But as we discussed in chapter 1, rulers should not be theocrats. That raises a difficult question. How should rulers discern between right and wrong without enforcing Christian belief and right worship? Should rulers not consult Scripture to discern right from wrong? If we say that the state has no institutional authority to enforce right belief, what standard of right and wrong should it consult?

Historically, the answer that most Christian theologians have given is *natural law*: a moral order evident in nature, inscribed into the created order of the universe, accessible to the rightly formed intellect, binding upon all humanity across time and culture. We can discern the natural law through reason unaided by revelation, which is why we can expect non-Christians to try to behave morally.

---

[20] Tacitus Agricola 30.4," in Neville Morely, *The Roman Empire: Roots of Imperialism* (London: Pluto, 2010), 38.

[21] Augustine, *City of God*, XIX. 12, 934.

Some Protestants may be wary of the language of natural law because it is, by reputation, a Roman Catholic property. That reputation is undeserved. Natural law is more pagan than Catholic in origin, as many pre-Christian philosophers, such as Aristotle and Cicero, appealed to some version of it. But some early church fathers embraced it, as did most of the Reformers. Protestants helped remind Christendom that unaided human reason is affected by the fall and, thus, is not a perfect guide: our understanding of natural law will be imperfect. Similarly, our will is fallen; even if we understand what nature demands, we are incapable of acting on it with perfect consistency and pure motives.[22]

Nonetheless, natural law is a biblical concept. In the Epistle to the Romans, Paul argues that those who reject God are still accountable to his law because "what can be known about God is evident among them, because God has shown it to them. For his invisible attributes, that is, his eternal power and divine nature, have been clearly seen since the creation of the world, being understood through what he has made. As a result, people are without excuse" (Rom 1:19–20). Paul expands on the idea in the next chapter: "So, when Gentiles, who do not by nature have the law, do what the law demands, they are a law to themselves, even though they do not have the law. They show that the work of the law is written on their hearts. Their consciences confirm this. Their competing thoughts either accuse or even excuse them" (Rom 2:14–15).

---

[22] Aquinas gets at something similar: "On account of the uncertainty of human judgment, especially on contingent and particular matters, different people form different judgments on human acts, whence also different and contrary laws result." ST, I–II, Q.91, A.4, in Aquinas, *On Law Morality and Politics*, 23.

Similarly, throughout the Old Testament, the prophets denounce Babylon, Assyria, and Egypt for oppression and tyranny even though those nations did not have the special revelation God gave to Israel. The prophets' jeremiads presuppose the pagan nations could understand the difference between right and wrong independent of Scripture. Paul, when debating the Athenians in their marketplace, appealed to their religious sensibilities and quoted their pagan poets, affirming the germ of something true in them. He argued that God made all nations "that they might seek God, and perhaps reach out and find him" (Acts 17:27). Paul was not arguing for universal salvation or suggesting all roads lead up the same mountain, but he was affirming that all humans are made in the image of God, that he made us with an inherent sense of him—or at least our need for him—and that to the extent we heed the law written on our hearts we are walking in the way God intended for us. All cultures reflect, imperfectly and with sinful distortions, grains of truth.

That is why there is good historical evidence for natural law. C. S. Lewis called it "the Tao" or "the Way" and documented in the appendix to *The Abolition of Man* that essentially every major religion and philosophy prohibits murder, lying, and theft. Most religions and philosophies exhort us to honor our elders and humble ourselves in the face of God, the gods, or the unknown.[23] These are statutes of the natural law. Natural law is how governments can govern righteously without governing theocratically. We know from Scripture that "righteousness exalts a nation, but sin is a disgrace to any people" (Prov 14:34). We also know from nature that

---

[23] C. S. Lewis, *The Abolition of Man* (Grand Rapids: Zondervan, 2001), appendix.

all rulers, everywhere, should pursue justice, peace, and order. That is, definitionally, what a government is.[24]

Ordered Liberty, Part 1

So far, we have reviewed basic concepts of political theology following the mainstream of Christian thought for millennia. I want to go a bit further. The argument I want to make is that natural law, rightly understood, leads us to embrace *ordered liberty* as a central organizing concept for just government.[25] If that is the case, we are led to some kind of representative, democratic, or republican form of government. This will be important for defining what counts as a *just cause* of war, and what justice after war looks like, in the next chapter. Christian political thought did not come to this conclusion until relatively recently—within the last 500 years or so—but this is an area in which I think we have seen genuine theological development. We should embrace this conclusion even as it departs from some of the great Christian thinkers of the past. Accountable government—at least of some kind—is rooted in natural law and biblical wisdom.

If there is a natural law, the golden rule is its first statute. Virtually every culture and religion has some version of the golden rule. Perhaps 500 years before Jesus, Confucius wrote "Never do to others what you would not like them to do to you."[26] In the

---

[24] See VanDrunen, *Politics after Christendom*, chap. 5, for a fuller discussion of natural law and its relationship to creation, the Noahic covenant, and civil government.

[25] For a fuller version of this argument, see chapters 6–7 in Paul D. Miller, *Just War and Ordered Liberty* (New York: Cambridge Univ. Press, 2021).

[26] Confucious, *The Analects of Confucius*, XV.23, trans. Arthur Waley (New York: Vintage, 1989), 198.

Mahabharata, the fifth-century-BC Hindu epic, one of the gods commands, "One should never do that to another which one regards as injurious to one's own self. This, in brief, is the rule of Righteousness."[27] These moral guidelines are so intuitive, engrained, and universal that we expect every human to understand and follow them, whether they have the Bible or not. The golden rule is the moral principle on which there is closest to a universal consensus across all lines of time, culture, and religion.

The golden rule is also the strongest argument for some form of accountable, participatory government, for an "open society" or a regime founded on liberty and equality. In short, the golden rule leads to some version of democracy or republicanism: they are the political version of the golden rule. (I am using "democracy" and "republicanism" as shorthand for the whole package of institutions that make up a free society.) In a democracy, I treat you as an equal citizen because I want you to treat me the same way. I recognize your rights and freedoms—free speech, free worship, and more—because I want you to recognize mine. I support equality under law for you and me alike. I support the rule of law—not the rule of a king's whim—because I do not want you to live under arbitrary rule any more than I want that for myself. I help protect your freedoms because I want you to protect mine.

Other political systems depend on unequal arrangements, on hierarchy: priest over layman; military over civilian; one race over another; one religion over another; one tribe, culture, tongue, or people over another. No such arrangement can survive the scrutiny of the golden rule because no emperor wants to be treated as a subject. Democracy is when the ruled are the rulers, when we treat others

---

[27] K. M. Ganguly, trans. *Mahabharata Anusasana Parva*, sec. CXIII, https://mahabharataonline.com/translation/mahabharata_13b078.php.

as the ruling ruled as they treat us likewise. If we take the political golden rule seriously, we must accept its full implications. When we recognize other people's right to say, to worship, and to print whatever they want, or we grant them equal citizenship and liberty, they are going to do and say things that we disagree with. The golden rule means we agree to live in a society with other people who will make choices we find objectionable, offensive, or even hateful.

This may sound, to some readers, novel—perhaps even too novel. Some readers may be suspicious that this is an intellectual and theological innovation, an exercise in twisting arguments to fit a predetermined conclusion. That is because we have been taught a faulty version of history. Most of us were taught that democracy or republicanism was invented by Enlightenment philosophers like John Locke and the Baron de Montesquieu, who pushed religion out of the public square first and rested their arguments for liberty and equality on an underlying premise of secularism.

In fact, the Christian case for republicanism starts with Jesus's commanding his followers, "Give, then, to Caesar the things that are Caesar's, and to God the things that are God's" (Matt 22:21), which later theologians formulated into the doctrines of the two swords or two kingdoms: the idea that the church and the state have separate jurisdictions and that the state's is not unlimited.[28] The idea of the state's limited jurisdiction and its accountability to a higher authority is the seedbed from which all the institutions of free, accountable

[28] On the "two kingdoms" concept, see David VanDrunen, *Natural Law and the Two Kingdoms: A Study in the Development of Reformed Social Though* (Grand Rapids: Eerdmans, 2009). The framework has been invoked for a variety of different purposes. Here, I simply note that it reflects Jesus's distinction between Caesar's authority and God's and that it *limits* Caesar's authority.

government eventually grew. Even at the height of Christendom, during which the church and state were unhealthily entwined, Christians still maintained an institutional distinction that was unusual compared to other religions in the world at the time.

The state's limited jurisdiction eventually led some to argue for the rights of conscience. Crucially, Enlightenment philosophers did not invent the argument and were not the first to make it. The argument for religious freedom was a theological argument from John Milton and Roger Williams before it was a secular argument from John Locke and Thomas Jefferson. (In fact, the first Christian ruler, the Roman Emperor Constantine, opted to make religious liberty—not Christian supremacy—his policy through the Edict of Milan in 313. It was a later emperor, Theodosius, who banned paganism and mandated Christianity.) Once we have religious freedom, the other basic freedoms—speech, association, press—follow as a matter of course.[29]

In fact, many of the Enlightenment philosophers' arguments were not secular at all. It is worth noting that, when Thomas Jefferson was making his argument for the American Revolution, he appealed to the authority of "the Laws of Nature and of Nature's God" in the Declaration of Independence.[30] Those were the ultimate justification for the "inalienable rights" he established as the bedrock of the American creed. Jefferson argued that natural law, as rooted in divine authority, taught that all are created equal and that the government should recognize that equality by respecting rights and

---

[29] See Robert Louis Wilken, *Liberty in the Things of God: The Christian Origins of Religious Freedom* (New Haven, CT: Yale Univ. Press, 2019).

[30] See "Declaration of Independence: A Transcription," July 4, 1776, on the National Archives website, America's Founding Documents, https://www.archives.gov/founding-docs/declaration-transcript.

allowing popular participation in government. Though Jefferson was hardly an orthodox Christian, his argument was steeped in Christian understanding, Christian wisdom, and Christian principles—and it is an argument Christians should continue to embrace today.

Governing as Gardening

Let us return to the Bible for a moment. I want to show how we can arrive at a similar place from a biblical starting point to reassure readers who may feel uncertain about the appeal to natural law. Let us return to the garden of Eden. In the Bible's opening chapters we see that God is king—and we are like God: "Then God said, 'Let us make man in our image, according to our likeness. They will rule the fish of the sea, the birds of the sky, the livestock' . . . So God created man in his own image, he created him in the image of God; he created them male and female" (Gen 1:26–27).

That is an astonishing claim and might sound arrogant if it were not true. In the ancient world, rich powerful men of the ruling tribe were sometimes said to be like the gods, but the idea that every human, male and female, rich and poor, slave and free was like God himself would have been scandalous. Indeed, the idea that we are all equal in the sight of God eventually led some Christians to argue that we should treat each other equally in this world. Some theologians have argued that the phrase "made *in* God's image" is better translated "made *as* God's image."[31] We are to be the image of God, to represent him, to the rest of creation. Earlier, in Genesis 1, God commanded humans to "be fruitful, multiply, fill the earth,

---

[31] D. J. A. Clines, "The Image of God in Man," *Tyndale Bulletin* 19, no. 1 (1968): 53–103, https://www.tyndalebulletin.org/article/30671-the-image-of-god-in-man.

and subdue it" (v. 28). We are his agents, his representatives, his vice-regents. We are to exercise dominion and stewardship over his creation on his behalf. God is king, and we are his lieutenants.

God gave his lieutenants a commission. He made a place specially designed for our flourishing and told us to take care of it. Think about the imagery here. God made everything, then takes a moment to *specially* plant the garden of Eden. A garden is different from a wilderness. A wilderness has no plan, no order to it. It is hard to survive in the wilderness. You do not know where or if you might find food. A garden, by contrast, is the wilderness tamed and brought under control; it is nature harnessed, channeled, and ordered to the needs and desires of the gardener. A wilderness might be grand, but it also might be dangerous and barren. A garden brings forth both nourishment and beauty: "The Lord God caused to grow out of the ground every tree pleasing in appearance and good for food" (Gen 2:9). In Genesis 2—before sin entered the world—God did not just plop us down into untamed wilderness to fend for ourselves. He carved out a special place of beauty and nourishment.

In planting a garden, God was also teaching us what our job was. He was the original gardener, planting Eden, but then he handed it over to us "to work it and watch over it" (Gen 2:15). Theologians have called Gen 2:15 the "cultural mandate." You may be wondering what gardening has to do with culture. Well, think of "agri-culture." It might be easier to think of this as the "cultivation" mandate. God has given us a commission to cultivate. We can cultivate the land, and we call it gardening or farming. But we can cultivate our minds, our communities, our human world, and we call it culture.

This is not just about gardening or farming. This is a commission for all our creative labor in all areas of our lives—including in governing. In a sense, Gen 2:15 is a description of what God originally intended our lives to be about before the fall. It is God's commission, authorization, and charge to us for what we are to do with our lives and how we are to relate to the rest of the world. This is a charge for your work—your work raising children, your work carrying out your paid employment, your work mentoring and discipling others, or your work serving our neighborhood, our church, our community, our country, and our world.

So, what does that "commission" mean? There are two parts to the commission. In various Bible translations, the specific verbs used, "tend" and "keep," can be translated "cultivate" and "keep" (NASB), "dress" and keep" (KJV), "work it and take care of it" (NIV), "tend" and "guard" and "keep" (AMPC), "work it and keep it" (ESV), "cultivate" and "guard" (GNT), and "till" and "keep" (NRSV).

The two parts of the commission are to (1) make it productive and (2) protect and watch over it. To make something productive, to *cultivate,* is to take something, prepare it for use, invest time and labor into making it yield its fruit, use it in a way that it generates growth and development and value. It is to sow labor, time, creativity, and love and to reap flourishing, beauty, nourishment, and fullness. To protect and watch over something is to be vigilant and attentive, to stand guard against danger from within and without, to walk the perimeter, maintain the boundaries, maintain a safe space within which the growth and fruitfulness can happen unhindered.

My wife and I kept a garden for the better part of a decade. I built raised garden beds from planks of wood, bought and mixed soil and manure. We positioned the garden to get the right mix of sun and shade. Together we and our kids tilled the soil, turning it to ensure a rich mixture of nutrients and creating lines in the dirt for orderly planting. We tied off string to create a grid and put the seeds into the soil at even intervals. We erected a trellis to give the plants a structure on which to grow. We put up a fence to keep pests out. We weeded the garden to protect the plants. We watered it on a regular schedule. Tending and keeping required us to take the raw stuff of nature and impose *order* upon it.

Then we stepped back and let the plants grow. At the end of the day, we could never *make* the plants grow; they grow by their given design from their Creator as reflected in their DNA and in the death and rebirth of seeds, in the life that only God can give. In all our gardening, we never actually created life, nor did we fashion anything new. We simply provided an orderly structure and gave life the *liberty* it needed to flourish, and we waited for life to take its course. Tending and keeping also means standing back. To tend and keep does not mean to control or micromanage or hover or be overbearing.

To act as God's vice-regent is to govern creation like a gardener. Governing a garden requires order and basic needs: soil, sunlight, and water, the bed, the orderly lines, the trellis. But it also requires liberty: stepping back, letting life take its course, recognizing that things have their own nature, understanding the nature of each plant and providing the resources and preconditions for its flourishing, but nothing more. Governing as gardening teaches that *life flourishes when given both order and liberty*. When God made humans and gave us a commission to be like him as vice-regents, stewards, and caretakers of his creation, he made us gardeners, tenders of a system of ordered liberty in which life flourishes.[32]

---

[32] This section is drawn from Paul Miller, "Ordered Liberty in the Bible," Initiative on Faith & Public Life, November 20, 2019, https://faithandpubliclife.com/ordered-liberty-in-the-bible/. VanDrunen reaches similar conclusions by appeal to the Noahic covenant. God renews the command to fill the earth and subdue it, which implies authorization to undertake a host of supporting activity for familial, "enterprise," and judicial institutions. This ultimately leads VanDrunen to make a case for limited government and "conservative liberalism." See VanDrunen, *Politics after Christendom*, chap. 3.

Ordered Liberty, Part 2

I want to respect Christian liberty and not make the Bible say something it does not say, so I want to be careful not to read too much of my own preferred political program into it. But the gardening metaphor and our reasoning from natural law seem to give us warrant for at least one statement of biblical politics: governments that respect the idea of *ordered liberty* are governing in a way most conducive to human flourishing—that is, with an eye toward *mishpat* and *tzadeqah*. And if governments should aim at creating and upholding a system of ordered liberty, Christians cannot and should not claim biblical warrant for any kind of total or complete order, nor for any kind of total or complete liberty.

The yearning for total order is behind authoritarian and tyrannical government, including theocracy, military dictatorships, totalitarian regimes, and other forms of authoritarian rule (and theocracy of course has other theological problems with it). The prophets were persistent in their condemnation of the nations for oppression. Not much has changed. Today we see the drive for total order alive and well around the world in dictatorial governments like China, Russia, North Korea, Iran, Saudi Arabia, and most of the Middle East.

The yearning for total liberty is expressed most purely in anarchism, which is rare today (though it was popular at the turn of the twentieth century). Some extreme forms of libertarianism come close to a theory of total liberty. But the best example of total "liberty" in actual practice is the sad reality of failed states. States like Somalia, Haiti (especially after the 2010 earthquake), and the Democratic Republic of the Congo lack any semblance of functioning government. The people can be said to be "free" of government, which might sound wonderful to those steeped in the Anglo-American tradition of distrust of government power. Yet we should leaven that tradition with biblical truth: government is ordained by God, and it is necessary for human life. The lack of governance is a moral failing and a deprivation of a fundamental good.

Does that mean the Bible supports democracy? Almost. The Bible *alone* does not quite get us there. It is more accurate to say that biblical wisdom, natural law, and a reasonable knowledge of history and human nature taken together virtually require us to support some version of accountable and limited government, which is best secured through democracy and civil liberties. Jonathan Leeman has helpfully made a distinction between different tiers of belief in political matters. He argues that there are certain absolute principles, called Tier 1 issues, like the sanctity of life, on which the Bible speaks clearly and which should bind our consciences. Tier 2 issues are those on which the Bible is less clear, or silent, and which are thus a matter of wisdom, prudence, and judgment, on which we should expect more latitude for disagreement. Leeman uses this distinction to say that life and justice are Tier 1, while the mechanisms and machinery of democracy are Tier 2.[33]

I want to use a modified version of this and make a slightly stronger case for democracy. As I argued above, the broad idea of *ordered liberty* is a biblical principle and thus a Tier 1 issue: Christians should never be on the side of tyrants or anarchists. The question is, What kind of institutions and mechanisms are best suited to achieve and sustain ordered liberty *across the generations*? I stress the last bit because it is a crucial part of the question typically unaddressed by critics of democracy.

---

[33] See Jonathan Leeman, *How the Nations Rage: Rethinking Faith and Politics in a Divided Age* (Nashville: Thomas Nelson, 2018).

Here is where I want to bring in evidence from history and social science, tools that allow us to come to more specific and concrete conclusions than if we restricted ourselves only to theological arguments. Based on theology alone, we cannot say much more than that governments ought to protect ordered liberty. But we can ask historians and social scientists: What regimes in history and practice have a proven record of safeguarding ordered liberty across the generations? There is, of course, only one answer: governments that are held accountable by some form of representation and elections and that are limited by some notion of fundamental rights and the rule of law. In short, republican or democratic regimes.

There may have been benevolent, enlightened monarchies or Caesaropapist regimes with a close church-state cooperation that upheld ordered liberty for a generation or two because of the charitable whim of an individual ruler, but they have always collapsed because they have no mechanism for the reliable transfer of power and because they lack the rule of law and the separation of powers necessary to keep bad rulers in check.

So, is democracy a Tier 1 or Tier 2 issue? I think of it as a Tier 1.5 issue because, although it is only an institutional mechanism for securing ordered liberty not explicitly mandated by Scripture, *we do not have an alternative, we never have, and we do not know of any other possible mechanism from history.* There are no other regimes that have ever successfully upheld and sustained ordered liberty *across the generations*. Since there are no alternatives, it seems foolish in the extreme to reject the one option we have. I am using "foolish" in the biblical sense: the Bible commands wisdom and condemns foolishness. Since we have been blessed to live at this time of history when we can consult the wisdom of the ages and see the evidence of democracy's performance over against the performance of every other type of regime, we would be culpably and possibly sinfully foolish to reject the institutions with the best track record for safeguarding *mishpat* and *tzadeqah* across the generations.

Conclusion

Let us bring these different strands of biblical political theology together.

1. From God's sovereignty, we learn that just rulers defend themselves, their rule, their people, and their realm. Just rulers punish rebels and uphold order. Just rulers love their people and work for their good and their flourishing.
2. From Israel's history and from the prophets, we see that justice and righteousness includes procedural justice, the impartial application of law, discernment between right and wrong, and restitution for wrongdoing; but also right relationships, attentiveness to the powerless, and some notion of inherent, individual dignity, even individual rights.
3. From the New Testament, we again see that government must uphold order and that order is a moral good (not a necessary evil). We also see that government must do justice: it must exercise judgment, punish the evildoer, give to everyone their due, and above all, recognize and be accountable to a standard of right and wrong that exists outside and above itself. To judge well without falling into the sin of theocracy, rulers should consult natural law.
4. Natural law, biblical wisdom, and knowledge of history and politics lead us to democracy, republicanism, or some form of an open society as the best set of institutions for upholding the closest approximation to *mishpat* and *tzadeqah* across the generations. No other form of government

> has the proven track record that democracy does, and it would be foolish to reject the best option we have.

These ideas have profound consequences for our understanding of justice and war. If war is to serve justice, it must serve to defend or reestablish sovereignty. But it must be a just sovereignty dedicated to order and peace, to *mishpat* and *tzadeqah*—which strongly suggests that, where possible, war should seek to defend, uphold, or restore institutions that protect human dignity and ordered liberty.

War is not about killing—killing is the necessary means of war, not its *telos* or purpose. The *telos* of war is a just peace, the reestablishment of a peaceful, ordered society in which all people are given their due, the right of the whole is protected alongside the rights of the individuals. As Augustine said, "The peace of all things lies in the *tranquility of order*; and order is the disposition of equal and unequal things in such a way as to give to each its proper place."[34] This is similar to Abraham Lincoln's vision of a "just and lasting peace" that should underlie any war that claims to be a just war. If war does not or cannot accomplish that, it is not a just war and can only result in an unjust peace, which is not true peace at all. "In comparison with the peace of the just," Augustine said, as noted earlier in the chapter, "the peace of the unjust is not worthy to be called peace at all."[35]

---

[34] Augustine, *City of God*, 936. Emphasis added.

[35] Augustine, 934.

3

The Just War Traditions

With a biblical understanding of justice and sovereignty, we can move on, finally, to war. When is war just? What does justice require? The just war tradition does not offer a single answer to these questions, in part because there *is not* a single just war tradition. The just war tradition has evolved over time, and different thinkers have offered different answers. Before we can walk through the criteria of just war thinking, a very brief overview of the history of just war thinking will help orient our discussion. Just war thinkers fall into three distinct sub-traditions: the Augustinian tradition, the Westphalian tradition, and the Liberal tradition.[1]

---

[1] See Paul D. Miller, *Just War and Ordered Liberty* (New York: Cambridge Univ. Press, 2021).

The Augustinian Tradition

The Augustinian just war tradition comes closest to resting on a biblical understanding of justice, though it needs some revision to apply to a twenty-first-century context. The Augustinian tradition took shape against the backdrop of Christendom, from antiquity through the late Medieval period. Augustine of Hippo (354–430) was the first (or most influential) to fuse crucial concepts inherited from pagan antiquity with Christian thought on natural law, justice, the state, and war. He did not, however, leave us a formalized just war doctrine. Later thinkers within the same tradition would further develop Augustine's thought, especially during the Wars of Religion.

Augustinian thinkers believed that natural law exists and should guide human social and political order to fulfill natural human moral aspirations. Sovereignty meant having responsibility for the common good. Justice sometimes required princes to use force to defend and uphold the common good. Just cause for war included not merely self-defense but also the defense of justice and peace, defense of the innocent, and punishment of the wicked. Statesmen were expected to wage war to defend the common good and, broadly, to uphold peace and justice, as understood by natural law. And statesmen were to fight war with the right intention: out of love for one's neighbor and one's enemies, not for glory, honor, revenge, or profit. Fighting to uphold justice and to prevent the wicked from perpetrating injustice was understood as the duty that Christian love required of statesmen.

The Augustinian tradition is unique in understanding war as an act of love. The statesman shows love by bringing the blessing of justice and order to his commonwealth and to his enemy alike. We can see the distinctive aspects of this approach most easily by examining how it deals with humanitarian intervention, revolt and rebellion, crimes against nature, and state building. Thinkers in the Augustinian tradition—especially the later thinkers who were more specific on these points—consistently prioritized the protection of the innocent, the pursuit of justice, and the preservation of just order. They generally favored what we would call humanitarian interventions: military operations to stop war crimes or crimes against humanity, to protect civilians, to punish tyrants and war criminals, and to foster conditions of lasting peace and stability. As such, thinkers in the Christian tradition stand in contrast to their Westphalian successors, for whom the norm of mutual noninterference among states assumed paramount importance.

The Westphalian Tradition

The Reformation fractured Christendom theologically. The ensuing Wars of Religion (1522–1648) fractured it politically and militarily. Protestant and Catholic powers fought to preserve, and sometimes impose, their faith under a close alignment between church and state. The conflicts culminated in the Thirty Years' War and ended with the Peace of Westphalia (1648). Neither side won. The peace settlement codified, not a victory by one side or the other, but an agreement that each ruler could impose his own religion within his own realm and would not seek to change the religion of other territories.

The social and political context that gave coherence to the Augustinian just war tradition was no more. A new tradition founded on a starkly different understanding of justice and sovereignty arose. The Westphalian system amounted to a realignment of religion and politics, a turning point in the development of modern nation states, and a symbolic end to wars fought over differences in religion. It changed the reasons that governments used to justify their wars.

The Westphalian tradition moved away from the Augustinian tradition in three respects: it was a tradition of legal reasoning, not political theology; its conception of natural law was descriptive, not teleological; and it tended to focus on procedural justice, not substantive justice. Together these innovations amounted to a change in the fundamental orientation of just war thinking. The Westphalian tradition left behind much of the theological background that had given the Augustinian tradition its content and meaning. For thinkers in the early modern and Enlightenment era, "natural law" meant something very different than it had meant for Augustine and his followers. Instead of a created moral order that guided rational creatures to fulfill their natures, natural law was closer to the law of the jungle. Self-preservation was its first statute.

The language of "just cause" and "right authority" also remained, but with transformed meanings. "Justice" was no longer the right ordering of all things and the "tranquility of order";[2] instead, justice meant abiding by the terms of a fictional "social contract" and the establishment of rights for individuals and for nations. "Sovereignty" evolved from responsibility for the common good to defense of international borders and even—given the new world of states competing in a zero-sum game for power and prestige following the law of self-preservation—license to maximize power. Just cause for war consequently shrank to encompass only territorial self-defense. The right authority for use of force was understood unproblematically to rest with the state, regardless of how the state chose to use it or for what purpose.

[2] Augustine, *The City of God* (New York: Random House), 690–91.

The Liberal Tradition

Westphalian sovereignty became the shield behind which dictators and tyrants could abuse and massacre their people with impunity. Without any sense of accountability to a higher power or to standards of conduct outside themselves, leaders came to see political power as self-justifying. The Holocaust violated no international law during the time in which it occurred. Because the world wars and the Holocaust discredited the most inflexible version of Westphalian sovereignty, they made plain the need to reintroduce some form of accountability for the behavior of states and the decisions of statesmen. The Nuremberg Trials of Nazi leaders were the first effort in history to hold government leaders criminally liable for acts of state.

At the same time, World War II was fought so indiscriminately, with millions of civilians killed through aerial bombardment, siege warfare, and starvation, that policymakers sought to strengthen the rules of warfare. They wanted militaries to show greater restraint and more respect for civilian life in line with the emerging democratic order that emphasized human rights and the sanctity of every individual. This amounted to the emergence of a new and still developing Liberal tradition of just war thinking. The embryonic Liberal tradition has arisen since World War II to rectify the weaknesses of the Westphalian tradition and, since the end of the Cold War, to address new and emerging security concerns, often by borrowing and reinterpreting Augustinian concepts shorn of their theological commitments.

In the Liberal tradition, concepts like human rights and accountable governance do the work that natural law and justice did in the Augustinian tradition when external standards outside and above the state were used to judge the state's legitimacy. War is just when it vindicates rights, not only the rights of states whose security has been violated, of course, but also the rights of individuals. The Liberal just war tradition (1) allows war when it is necessary to vindicate the rights of individuals suffering under a humanitarian emergency, (2) insists on respecting individual rights in how war is fought, and (3) understands that the vindication of individual rights is a crucial part of ending wars justly.

Which tradition is right? Which is the best reflection of a biblical understanding of justice and the purposes of government? The Augustinian tradition emerged first and was most self-consciously trying to offer a Christian answer. But the Augustinian tradition was rooted in the world of Christendom, including a church-state relationship that was more indebted to pagan antiquity than biblical fidelity. The Liberal tradition, despite disavowing any sectarian or theological commitments, reflects a more Christian understanding of religious disestablishment. However, the Liberal tradition on its own is rootless and has only a shallow understanding of justice. The best approach—the most faithful to biblical political theology—is an Augustinian Liberalism, or a Liberal Augustinianism, one that combines the best and most biblically faithful aspects of each. It is this synthesis that informs the rest of this book.

The Just War Categories

The ethics of warfare is an enormously complex topic. The just war tradition helps break it down into three broad categories of questions: justice *before*, *during*, and *after* war.[3]

[3] For a similar overview of the just war categories, see Eric Patterson, *A Basic Guide to the Just War Tradition* (Grand Rapids: Baker, 2023).

1. When is war just? What are just reasons to go to war? Who gets to decide?
2. How do we fight war justly? What are the rules that should guide the conduct of warfare?
3. What does a just outcome of war look like? What should be the hoped-for goal or aim that we seek to achieve in the aftermath of war?

Because the discussion was formalized by Medieval theologians, the categories naturally have Latin names: *jus ad bellum* (the justice *of* war); *jus in bello* (justice *in* war); and *jus post bellum* (justice *after* war). Each has its own subcategories.

Table 3.1: The Just War Criteria	
Jus ad bellum (moral considerations)	Just Cause
	Right Authority
	Right Intention
Jus ad bellum (prudential considerations)	Reasonable Chance of Success
	Last Resort
	Proportionality in Ends
Jus in bello	Proportionality in Means
	Discrimination
	Military Necessity
Jus post bellum	Order
	Justice
	Conciliation

Jus ad Bellum *(The Justice of War)*

When is war just? Who gets to declare war? The first question to consider is *jus ad bellum* (the justice *of* war): the justice of why the war is fought, by whom, and for what reason. Traditionally, theologians focused on moral consideration, including *just cause*, *right authority*, and *right intention*. More recently, some thinkers have proposed prudential criteria, including (1) having a reasonable chance of success, (2) waging war only as a last resort, and (3) ensuring that the expected benefits are proportional to the expected costs of war.

Just Cause

A just war must be fought for a just cause; or to put it another way, it must be fought for justice, not for glory, conquest, bloodlust, or plunder. Of course, to say that war must be fought for justice simply invites the question, What is justice? This is the most contentious question of the just war tradition, and various thinkers have sometimes been vague or inconsistent on this point. Augustine's standard, for example, is fuzzy: he says that just war must be a response to an injury received. What kind of injury? At what scale? By whom, against whom? Is the injured party the only one who can respond, or can others respond on the injured's behalf? Does the injury have to take place across international borders?

Later thinkers would provide specific, diverging, and sometimes expansive lists of just causes for war, including: to defend the true faith, to enforce the right of free passage, to enforce the right to proselytize, to defend against invasion, to recover stolen property, to exact recompense for damages, to deter future wrongdoing, to vindicate honor, to preserve the balance of power, to defend the innocent, to defend one's rights, to defend human rights generally, to punish the wicked, to punish crimes against nature, to stop genocide, and more.

That is why it is important to begin with a biblical understanding of justice and government's authority. Drawing from the previous chapter, we can answer that if justice is *mishpat* and *tzadeqah*—the justice of rights, process, and law as well as the justice of reconciliation, right relationships, and flourishing—the government must wield the sword to defend, restore, and vindicate *mishpat* and *tzadeqah* when they are under violent attack. This is not only a doctrine of just *war* but of just *force* generally. All the government's coercive powers, including military force abroad and policing at home, derive from this idea. When *mishpat* or *tzadeqah* is violated by individual criminals or criminal organizations at home, the police and the judicial system rightfully seek to bring them to justice—including, if necessary, with armed force—and to achieve restitution for victims. Policing is a just and necessary use of physical force to uphold order and pursue justice.

The same principle applies internationally. When one nation invades another—as when Germany invaded Poland in 1939, the Soviet Union invaded Afghanistan in 1979, or Russia invaded Ukraine in 2022—that constitutes a massive violation of the invaded nation's *mishpat* and a disruption of the *tzadeqah* that should hold among nations. Resisting such an invasion is the rightful prerogative—the duty, in fact—of the victims to restore *mishpat* for itself and *tzadeqah* for all nations. Self-defense against invasion is the clearest and easiest case of just war.

But most military operations are not so clear cut as defending against attempted conquest. What about preemptive or preventive war? In 1967, Israel attacked Egypt, claiming it was an act of self-defense to preempt an imminent attack by Egypt and its allies. In 2003, the United States invaded Iraq under a similar rationale, arguing that Iraq was pursuing weapons of mass destruction and, if successful, would pose a threat to the whole world. Were either of these wars justified?

The just war traditions (all of them) have generally agreed that preemptive war is justifiable *in principle* yet extremely difficult to justify *in practice*. If you see the brawler winding up to throw the first punch, you do not have to wait for it to land on your face before defending yourself. If a mugger pulls a gun, you do not have to wait for him to pull the trigger. You are allowed to shoot first.

But consider: the knowledge that preemptive defense is justified might tempt you to be trigger-happy, prone to see threats that are not there or to feel threats to be more imminent than they really are. Was the man really winding up for a punch, or just gesticulating passionately? Was that a gun, or a cellphone? Justified preemption depends on correctly predicting the future, on accurately divining our enemy's capabilities and intentions, but there is little in history to suggest we are good at doing that. Israel's justified preemptive attack in 1967 is the rare exception to the general rule. The war in Iraq illustrates the more typical case, that we rarely understand our enemy as well as we think.

What about armed interventions to stop state failure, war crimes, genocide, or other crimes against humanity? Was it just for the United States to intervene in the Balkans to stop ethnic cleansing and civil war in the 1990s? Or to intervene in Libya to prevent a likely massacre in 2011? Should it have intervened in Rwanda to stop genocide in 1994? What looks like a humanitarian intervention by well-meaning outsiders might look like a war of invasion and conquest by those on the other end. Which takes precedence: the principle of sovereignty or the principle of human rights?

This is a question on which the just war traditions are split. The Westphalian tradition answers that sovereignty matters more and humanitarian interventions are not justified. The Augustinian and Liberal traditions give the opposite answer: they endorse the principle of humanitarian intervention, which seems closer to a biblical understanding of justice, sovereignty, and the purpose for which God authorized the sword. At some point, a government that is unusually murderous and tyrannical is no longer a government. Intervening is not a war of conquest but a police action against an international criminal gang posing as a state.

What about rebellion and civil war? When, if ever, is rebellion justified? Was the American Revolution justified in 1776? Or the French in 1789? Or the Russian in 1917? Who had justice on their side in the Syrian civil war? Or the American Civil War? Was it just for South Sudan to secede from Sudan in 2011, Eritrea from Ethiopia in 1991, or the Soviet Socialist Republics from the USSR the same year? Or the various Balkan states from Yugoslavia in 1992? Can outsiders support rebels, as the US tried with Nicaraguan rebels in the 1980s and Syrian rebels in 2010s? What about the dozens of wars of national liberation against imperial powers that littered the twentieth century?

These are extraordinarily difficult questions, and they lead directly to the next question: Who is authorized to wage war?

Right Authority

Who is allowed to declare and wage war? Who is allowed to initiate, lead, or decide upon war? Biblically, God commissions governments, not individuals, to wield the sword. All versions of the just war tradition agree. The just war tradition first reached maturity in the high Middle Ages when theologians were concerned about the prevalence of warlords, duels, private warfare, banditry, and quasi-governmental wars by lesser lords. They argued that only the prince or ruler and his legitimately constituted military forces have the right authority to undertake warfare.

That would seem to leave no room for justified rebellion, insurgency, or civil war, and the Westphalian tradition generally frowns on any argument in favor of rebellion or civil war. However, the Augustinian and Liberal traditions again chart a different path and open a narrow pathway for justified revolt. Why?

As before, the question to ask is, What happens when governments fail to be governments? Though all governments are flawed and show evidence of corruption, incompetence, or oppression as a normal feature of human political life in a sinful world, there are also rare cases in history of governments that show an exceptional degree of barbarity and cruelty—institutions that claim to be governments but show, through their actions, that they are little more than criminal gangs of murderers or slavers.

In those cases, there is a vacuum of legitimate sovereign authority amid massive, systemic violations of *mishpat* and *tzadeqah*—what the Augustinian just war tradition used to call "crimes against nature"—by criminals pretending to be governments. In those rare cases, the right authority to wield the sword passes downward, to the people, and outward, to other nations, who may fight against a murderous or enslaving regime to reconstitute competent public authority. The Germans who tried unsuccessfully to resist the Nazi regime were not guilty of sedition because, in a real sense, there was no legitimate German government and no German was obligated to obey the Nazi regime's criminal orders.

The same answer applies to cases of state failure. In cases not of tyranny but of anarchy, when governments have ceased to function—as in large parts of Somalia, Afghanistan, and the Democratic Republic of the Congo in the 1990s—both the population and other nations may wield the sword to reconstitute a sovereign authority—though if outsiders do intervene, it must be in deference to and support of local actors and with the ultimate aim of handing sovereignty over to them.

One more contemporary issue complicates the discussion of right authority. Today some have argued that right authority no longer belongs to individual governments but should be vested in the United Nations (UN) or, perhaps, some other organization or coalition like the North Atlantic Treaty Organization (NATO). While we can affirm the wisdom of one nation seeking the accountability, counsel, and oversight of other, trustworthy nations or of working through established avenues of cooperation, no institution or coalition carries the same biblical mandate that governments do. Sovereign governments alone have the mandate to wield the sword. Again, there is a strong degree of wisdom in several nations consulting together before deciding how and when to wield it, but no authority exists outside or above sovereign nations to veto their decisions.

I would simply add that institutions like the UN do not gain more moral authority by having universal membership; rather, the opposite is more likely true. The UN's decision-making process is compromised by the inclusion of some states—like Russia, China, and North Korea—that are themselves among the worst violators of *mishpat* and *tzadeqah* in the world. We should seek accountability and wisdom from a small number of trusted friends whose judgment is tested and proven and not give an equal say to every single person, including criminals, bullies, and fools. If and when the United States seeks multilateral consultation about war, it should consult with its democratic allies first and foremost.

Right Intention

It is important not only that rulers have just cause for war but also that they carry out war with the right motives. Early Christian just war thinkers, such as Augustine and Aquinas, were concerned, pastorally, for the state of rulers' hearts and the hearts of the soldiers who fought war. They were aware that, even when just, war tempts rulers and soldiers to rage, vindictiveness, murder, bigotry, theft, rape, and more. Just warriors must fight with the right heart. They may not use a just cause, such a repelling an invasion, as a pretext for indulging bloodlust, exacting revenge, or committing war crimes.

Right intention is a strange criterion to talk about today because the just war framework is often presented in secular or legal terms. Talking about people's heart motives does not fit those categories. The Westphalian tradition made little use of the concept. The oddness should be a reminder that the church has an important role discipling and counseling members who participate in war as decision-makers, soldiers, or even just as spectators, regardless of how the world talks about just war (see chapter 6).

Pastors, priests, and elders should be prepared to counsel soldiers about to go on deployment to help them examine their hearts and guard against the temptations inherent in combat. With the aid of informed experts, they should counsel their congregations about how to pray, think, and feel about wars their nations are involved in. And they should be prepared to offer counseling for soldiers returning from combat to process their experience. Simply talking about their experience in war with trusted friends, family, and spiritual counselors can help soldiers understand whether and to what extent they acted rightly, and thus be at peace with their actions, and to what extent they may need to repent for sin. Either way, post-combat counseling can help soldiers prevent or cope with post-traumatic stress disorder and transition to peacetime and civilian life.

But right intention is not only a reminder for counseling at the individual level. It is also a call to accountability at the national level. Today's governments are corporate entities. The inner heart motivation of any one politician, general, soldier, or bureaucrat is rarely the deciding factor in setting policy or strategy. In the context of the modern bureaucratic state, the appropriate way to measure right intention is by examining the state's war aims, its policy choices, and the fruit of its actions. We should ask: Will the war result in justice and peace? Does the government's strategy aim at producing justice and peace, or are those just rhetorical flourishes, fig leaves to cover more limited and selfish aims? These questions lead us to ask about justice *after* war, which we will take up below under the *jus post bellum* category.

Reasonable Chance of Success, Proportionality, and Last Resort

Before we conclude this part of the discussion, we should note that some contemporary scholars have argued for additional *jus ad bellum* criteria: war must be a last resort, must have a reasonable chance of success, and must be proportional to the ends sought. These are more practical than theological considerations; they are specific and intuitive applications of broader principles of wisdom. War is terrible. We should not rush to war, we should minimize its destruction, and we should seek alternatives when possible. In Deut 20:10, God commands Israel, "When you approach a city to fight against it, make an offer of peace" and to go to war only if peace terms are rejected. We should work hard to avoid war and never fight needlessly.

Those are true, of course. But the specific criteria can be unhelpful in assessing the justice of a war beforehand because they seem to require an unattainable degree of knowledge and control of future events. War and politics are unpredictable. As soon as a war begins, it changes things. It is impossible for any political leader, at the outset, to fully and accurately foresee how a war will play out, what its costs and benefits will be, and thus what its chance of success is or its sense of proportionality. The proverbial fog and friction of war is an intrinsic part, not only of combat but also of our knowledge and agency in wartime.

Of course, we should use all the wisdom, knowledge, and expertise at our disposal, and leaders should not launch wars without thinking through the likely consequences. The problem is not that these prudential criteria are wrong—they are not—but that they are not *useful*—that is, they cannot be used or applied in practical debate about a specific case. For example, take the 2003 war in Iraq. The Bush administration claimed that war was a last resort because of the Iraqi regime's long record of violating UN Security Council Resolutions and because it had ejected international weapons inspectors. The administration's critics claimed that Bush should have given diplomacy more time, given Iraq another chance to comply with sanctions and inspections, or given the UN one more chance to enforce its resolutions.

But asking either side for their best argument is to invite them to commit one or another logical fallacy or cognitive error. Asking political leaders to assess whether a proposed war is truly a last resort incentivizes wishful thinking and motivated reasoning. Under pressure to show that they have done all they can, leaders may be tempted to paint an overly rosy picture or cherry-pick evidence from history to support their case (as critics say was the case with the Bush administration). On the other hand, critics of a war can lapse into a functional pacifism by insisting to give peace one more chance, and then one more after that. In one sense, war is never truly a last resort because there is always the option not to fight at all. It is possible to avoid all wars by simply acceding to the demands of any aggressor. Surrender is an effective pathway to peace, though not a just or honorable peace.

While we should hope and pray that war is indeed a last resort, demanding proof that it is or is not a last resort does not serve to inform or structure public debate in any meaningful way. As long as there are plausible alternatives to war for defending peace and justice, leaders should pursue them. But we should not let hair-splitting over whether they have truly reached the "last resort" become an excuse for paralysis, inaction, and dereliction of duty.

The same is true of the other prudential criteria. The Bush administration claimed that the war in Iraq would be proportional and had a reasonable chance of success because they believed the war would be quick and relatively low-cost. Critics complained, especially after the fact, that policymakers failed to anticipate exactly what would happen during the war or how costly it turned out to be. The critics were right—but that is hardly surprising. The problem is less that the administration got their prediction wrong than that they tried to make a prediction in the first place. It is folly to try to tally up in advance how many bombs, bullets, dollars, and troops a war will cost. Every war takes unexpected turns and almost always ends up costing more than anticipated. Asking leaders to make such predictions creates an unrealistic and unachievable expectation that war will conform to our plans.

As a famous military aphorism puts it, no plan survives first contact with the enemy (or everyone has a plan until you are punched in the face). Plans are important more for the intellectual habit of anticipation, flexibility, and preparedness they foster in the minds of commanders and decision-makers than for any ability they have to force events to conform to our will. Asking for a net assessment (counting up future costs and benefits and offering a conclusion about the war's chances of success like a math problem) fosters an unhelpful expectation that military planning and strategy will have a high degree of precision and predictive power that they simply cannot have.

Jus in Bello *(Justice in War)*

Once war has begun, another set of questions arise: How do we fight war justly? What does justice require of us during war? *Jus in bello* is "justice in war," the justice of how we fight. Simply put, we should be careful whom we kill and how much violence we use.

Discrimination

In a just war, we must carefully discriminate between legitimate military targets, such as enemy soldiers, equipment, and military facilities, and everyone and everything else, which we must strive to protect even amid the chaos of war. The prohibition on targeting civilians extends to the stuff civilians depend on for their lives. "When you lay siege to a city for a long time, fighting against it in order to capture it, do not destroy its trees by putting an ax to them . . . ," God commanded Israel. "Are trees in the field human, to come under siege by you?" (Deut 20:19). Militaries may not deliberately target infrastructure that exists solely for civilian use, such as medical facilities, farmland, schools, or religious buildings. (If the enemy hides in them or uses them to store weapons, as Hamas does, those facilities become legitimate military targets—though that does not mean it is always *prudent* to use force against them.)

War is not an excuse for indiscriminate killing, an ideal noteworthy for how rarely humanity has observed it. Genghis Khan was infamous for ordering the enslavement or execution of every man, woman, and child in the cities he conquered across Asia in the twelfth and thirteenth centuries. In 1631, during the Thirty Years' War, the Catholic League destroyed the city of Magdeburg, Germany, incinerating its buildings and killing nearly all its 25,000 inhabitants, defenders and civilians alike. World War II was probably the apex of indiscriminate warfare in history, as all sides bombed civilian targets during the war, including the Allies' firebombing of dozens of German and Japanese cities late in the war. The Nazis were, of course, much worse. They starved up to one million Russian civilians during just one operation—the siege of Leningrad—and deliberately murdered six million Jewish civilians in a campaign of genocide.

Such mass atrocities are obviously wrong, and that style of indiscriminate warfare has almost entirely disappeared since World War II. Most rich-world militaries now require military targeting to go through a lengthy process to demonstrate that a proposed air strike or military operation will be a small as possible, will not deliberately target civilians, and will minimize the risk of accidental harm to civilians and civilian infrastructure, a process helped enormously by the advent of precision-guided munitions, one of the greatest advances in the moral technology of warfare in history. Ground combat today typically has stricter rules of engagement than previously, though those are harder to sustain and protracted ground combat seems to wear those guardrails down, as some examples from America's war in Vietnam show.

Some countries never adapted to a higher standard of discrimination, however, as shown by the Soviet Union's ghastly war in Afghanistan in the 1980s—which killed, wounded, or displaced half the country—and Russia's war against Ukraine in 2022. The Global South still witnesses indiscriminate warfare—the Great African War (1998–2003) may have killed nearly six million people—though civilian deaths are just as often from disease and starvation as from direct violence.

Much harder to assess are the choices individual soldiers must make in tactical situations where it is unclear who the enemy is. During the wars in Iraq and Afghanistan, American and allied soldiers often patrolled in towns or cities alongside Afghan or Iraqi policemen and soldiers amid local civilians. Insurgents wearing no uniform would hide among the population (itself a war crime) to plant a bomb or launch an ambush. After a firefight, insurgents would flee, hide their weapons, and pretend to be civilians. In those circumstances, soldiers—whether Afghan, Iraqi, American, or Allied—would have to make difficult decisions about who was a legitimate target, whom they were allowed to arrest or shoot, or when they should show restraint and let insurgents go rather than risk killing civilian bystanders.

In 2007, General David Petraeus introduced a counterinsurgency strategy in Iraq. General Stanley McChrystal followed suit in Afghanistan in 2009, both following ideas General Creighton Abrams innovated in Vietnam after 1969. Petraeus's strategy emphasized protecting the population over killing enemy combatants. Petraeus argued that the US and the Iraqi government could not kill their way to victory; rather, they had to win the population's trust, rebuild the Iraqi government, and invest in lasting conditions of peace. Historians will argue for decades whether the strategy was more effective (I think it clearly was), but it seems obvious from a just war standpoint that the counterinsurgency strategy was a commendable effort to err on the side of greater discrimination, to protect lives, and to minimize war's destructiveness.

Proportionality and Military Necessity

In war, soldiers must use means—tactics and weapons—that are proportionate to the end they are trying to accomplish.[4] What does proportionality mean? It means that we may not use a nuclear weapon to take out a sniper. We cannot bulldoze an entire village to find one insurgent. It means that we must calibrate our weapons, tactics, and targets to the military requirements of the mission, and no more. Broadly, we may not use excessively brutal, dehumanizing, or vindictive means to achieve our end.

That invites the question, What counts as "excessive"? This requires two elaborations. First, proportionality does *not* mean that we get to kill the precise number of enemy soldiers as they killed on our side. Some people misunderstand proportionality as a blanket permission to be as brutal and bloodthirsty as the enemy. Proportionality is not a way of restating the "eye for an eye" ethic of Leviticus 24, as if war is justified as long as we get *a body for a body, a kill for a kill.* If a terrorist bomb kills a dozen civilians, that does not mean we have permission to kill a dozen terrorists—no more, no less—in retaliation. The goal in war is never the death of our enemies but the achievement of peace and justice. Killing the enemy is the necessary and regrettable means when they violently resist, but "don't gloat when your enemy falls" (Prov 24:17). God

---

[4] This is different from proportionality of the war as a whole, discussed above. Both are important, but proportionality *in bello* is easier to judge with accuracy.

tells us that "I take no pleasure in the death of the wicked" (Ezek 33:11). If we can achieve justice with zero deaths, that is the proportional response.

The proportionality we seek is not about the body count but about the scale of destruction we are forced to inflict compared to the impact it will have on the likelihood of victory and, ultimately, compared to the scale of peace and justice we seek to build. If an act has only a small impact on the military situation yet inflicts mass casualties—even of legitimate military targets—it is disproportionate. In 1991, President George H. W. Bush ordered the US military to stop bombing the "Highway of Death" as Iraqi soldiers fled Kuwait, in part because he judged the war was effectively won and further killing was unnecessary, even though the Iraqi government had not surrendered yet and the soldiers in question were still technically legitimate targets.

But there is another way of misunderstanding proportionality. On the other end of the spectrum, some misunderstand it to mean that we must restrain ourselves at every point, that anything approaching "total war" is necessarily disproportionate, and that we can only use "normal" weapons and tactics. None of this makes sense. Proportionality does not mean we must avoid weapons and tactics that make people feel squeamish, and it does not necessarily require us to lose a war for the sake of the moral high ground. War is, by its nature, brutal and inhuman. Winning requires being more brutal than your enemy. Some of the "laws of war" amount to trying to make killing more gentlemanly, which denies the reality of what war already is. All war is inhumane, which means there is a virtue in fighting it so effectively as to end it as quickly as possible.

This is a tricky argument. Policymakers and historians often argue over whether some specific act of brutality—waterboarding a detainee, dropping a nuclear weapon on Hiroshima, or General

William Tecumseh Sherman's "march to the sea" in 1864—was necessary to break the enemy's will and win the war. Some argue that wars seem to end definitively only when the enemy nation feels defeated, which requires total war. On the other hand, critics of this view argue that total war violates proportionality and is always wrong. Advocates of total war respond that, if so, then the requirement for proportionality itself is the problem because it undermines the brutality necessary for victory. Which is the right answer: proportional, restrained warfare that risks losing, or unrestrained war that has a higher chance of winning at the cost of the last remnants of our humanity?

I dislike the framing because it presumes a conflict between morality and victory. In a just war, it is just to win. There should be no conflict between what is just and what is strategically wise. Some scholars have helpfully tried to recast the argument around "military necessity."[5] Assuming the war we are fighting is just, it is just to use the weapons and tactics required to achieve victory—no more and no less—because victory in a just cause is a moral imperative.

If nuclear weapons were necessary to defeat Japan and end the most catastrophic war in all history, as I believe they probably were, then that is a strong argument that they were justifiably proportional (although there is a separate question about whether nuclear weapons pass the test of discrimination, given how many civilians were killed). The US military and intelligence agencies argued at the time that Japan was unlikely to surrender—based on the emperor's public statements and the previous three years' experience fighting Japanese forces that rarely surrendered—and that an

---

[5] See Eric D. Patterson, "Military Necessity, Proportionality, and Discrimination," in *The Ethics of Urban Warfare: City and War*, ed. Dragan Stanar and Kristina Tom (Boston: Brill, 2023).

invasion of Japan would kill millions. If, however, Japan could have been compelled to surrender without the use of nuclear weapons (which seems unlikely) and without significantly extending the war or causing even more casualties on both sides, then nuclear weapons would have been disproportionate and unjust.

These are disputed *historical* questions, and that is the right focus of debate. To assert, independent of the historical context, that the bombing of Hiroshima was obviously just, or obviously unjust, on the grounds of the killing being proportionate or disproportionate is to miss the morally relevant facts of the case. Moral reasoning deals with abstract concepts like "justice," but passing specific moral judgments requires careful historical knowledge. In other words, we cannot judge that total war is always right or always wrong: it depends on whether total war is *necessary for victory*. It virtually never is. Almost all wars in history are limited wars that do not justify unlimited means.

But World War II was indeed a total war, and I am inclined to believe the atomic bombings were necessary to win the war quickly without invading Japan. That does not give the US blanket permission to bomb indiscriminately, however, and I would also criticize how the military picked targets and its evident lack of concern for minimizing civilian casualties throughout the strategic bombing campaign, including at Hiroshima and Nagasaki. Using the bomb in combat against Japan was probably necessary and certainly better than the alternatives, but US officials could have at least tried to pick a better target that minimized civilian casualties.[6]

---

[6] For a fuller discussion of that case, see Francis X. Winters, *Remembering Hiroshima: Was It Just?* (New York: Routledge, 2016). I do not agree with all of Winters's conclusions, but he covers the historical and ethical ground well.

The moral quality of war inheres in its purpose and its relationship to justice and peace, not in specific weapons or tactics, our visceral response, or whether something counts as "total war." We sometimes overfocus on attention-getting incidents in our debates about war. Another illustration involving weapons of mass destruction is helpful here. When Bashar al-Assad used chemical weapons against Syrian rebels in 2012 and 2013, President Barack Obama initially argued that was a "red line" that should have triggered international action because chemical weapons were especially pernicious, barbaric, and inhumane (he later backed off). But Assad's chemical weapons had killed dozens or perhaps hundreds of Syrians while normal bullets and explosives had already killed a half-million people in the previous several years of war. The Interahamwe militia murdered up to one million Rwandans in 1994 with machetes. Assad's chemical weapons were not morally worse—they were no more disproportionate—than Assad's bullets or the Interahamwe's blades.

Jus post Bellum *(Justice after War)*

How do we achieve justice after war? In one sense, this is the most important question. If a war does not achieve peace and justice, little else matters. A war might be justly begun and justly fought, but if it ends only in destruction and misery, it cannot be called a just war in any meaningful sense (which may be, sadly, the appropriate verdict on both World War I and the Iraq War).

Yet the just war traditions rarely treated justice after war as a distinct question. Some scholars in the Augustinian tradition addressed what to do after war, but they did so under the heading of right intention. For example, they would argue that a king's righteous intentions would bear fruit in the magnanimity and wisdom he would show in a war's conclusion: he would treat defeated enemies with mercy, honor treaties, treat prisoners well, etc. Scholars began treating justice after war as a separate category only in the 1990s, probably out of concern for that era's proliferation of post-conflict stability operations (which were often not truly *post*-conflict at all). Today, Eric Patterson has offered the best framework for *jus post bellum*. Patterson argues that policymakers must strive for order, justice, and conciliation.[7]

Order

Little else is possible in a society that lacks a sense of public order. War disrupts public order, but order does not automatically snap back into place when war ends, particularly in a defeated country. Disorder is often rampant. Government may or may not exist; if it does, it may be too weak to enforce laws. The local police might have been drafted into the army and thus decimated or scattered after defeat; or they might simply not show up to work after a war's end. Returning soldiers might turn to crime, warlordism, and trafficking to support themselves. They might organize themselves into insurgent or terrorist cells to take revenge on the enemy or on their own countrymen whom they deem insufficiently loyal. If disorder and poverty linger, political extremism can take root and threaten long-term peace.

It is the responsibility of victors to restore order. This is not a new requirement of modern just war thinking nor the invention of idealists and utopians. It is a basic, commonsense, universal consensus of all just war traditions with centuries of precedent. Especially

---

[7] See Eric D. Patterson, *Ending Wars Well: Order, Justice, and Conciliation in Cotemporary Post-Conflict* (New Haven, CT: Yale Univ. Press, 2012).

in the aftermath of the wars in Iraq and Afghanistan, some scholars and policymakers deride any post-conflict operations as "nation building" and argue that outside powers have no business staying involved after a war. Kill the bad guys and leave, or as the British used to say, "butcher and bolt," which is more or less what the US and its allies did in Libya in 2011. Such a view may have an intuitive appeal, especially for those skeptical of our ability to do post-conflict operations well.

While post-conflict operations are certainly complex and difficult and there is a legitimate debate about how much and what kind of post-conflict operations are required, there is no justification for abandoning a defeated country in a state of anarchy. If we fight a just war out of love for our enemies, that love will show up in how we treat them in the aftermath. If we fight to defend peace and justice, we will invest in lasting conditions of order as the essential precondition for peace and justice to take root. From the perspective of the just war traditions—any of them—"butcher and bolt" is a morally bankrupt, indefensible position with no basis in Scripture, theology, or natural or international law.

Depending on the severity of the war, the restoration of order in its aftermath may require military forces to police streets, detain former combatants and common criminals, process a large number of prisoners of war, assist in the reconstitution of civil authority, train new police and military forces, and more. That is not required after every war—most wars do not result in regime collapse and the complete breakdown of order on one side or the other. But consider even a war like the Russo-Ukraine war that started in 2014 and escalated in 2022. Ukraine has been devasted, much of its infrastructure destroyed. An alarming number of soldiers and security forces have been killed or wounded. If, as we pray, the war ends (it is ongoing at the time of this writing) and Ukraine emerges still independent, it is likely to grapple with poverty, crime, and lawlessness because of the weakness of its institutions and security forces. International assistance to keep order in Ukraine will be essential to putting the country back together.

Justice

War is a response to a wrong committed. A just war, at minimum, corrects the wrong that started the war. Just war *gives judgment.* It gives to each their due: to the aggressor, punishment; to the victim, restitution. It seeks to rectify wrongs, restore rights, provide compensation, and reestablish the normal procedures of diplomacy and dispute adjudication. A just war reestablishes *mishpat.*

Iraq invaded Kuwait in 1990; the war ended with the liberation of Kuwait. The Soviet Union invaded Afghanistan in 1979; the war ended with its withdrawal ten years later. Those withdrawals were the minimum condition of justice. World War I ended with Germany's defeat, the liberation of occupied territories, and the restoration of the United States' maritime rights (the cause of the US's intervention in the war). In that sense, World War I was perhaps minimally just—though in the next section, on conciliation, we will see how far it fell short of a fuller sense of justice.

Often, because this is a fallen world, we must speak of gradations or degrees of justice. Russia invaded Ukraine and annexed the Crimean Peninsula in 2014, then invaded the rest of the country in 2022. A perfectly just end to that war would include a complete Russian withdrawal and restoration of all territory to Ukraine, coupled with Russian reparations paid to Ukraine. An end to the war that recognizes Ukrainian independence but allows Russia to keep Crimea or territory in the eastern Donbas region would be less just, or partially just and partially unjust. A Russian victory and the complete annexation of Ukraine would be perfectly unjust. Sadly, policymakers often are forced to deal in and accept partially just solutions because those are the only realistic options.

Just wars also seek justice for wrongs done *during* war. War invariably invites war crimes, unnecessary force, collateral damage, civilian deaths, and often—as Russia and Hamas have amply and horribly demonstrated—deliberate murder, rape, and theft. Holding soldiers and decision-makers accountable, insofar as possible, and providing restitution to victims are other crucial parts of *post bellum* justice. The Nuremberg Trials of Nazi leaders set a precedent that government leaders would be held personally and criminally liable for war crimes, a precedent that has helped increase oversight and accountability for militaries, at least among democratic countries.

What happens when the war's cause changes? When the "wrong" in response to which the war is waged changes mid-war? The secession of Southern states was the immediate trigger of the American Civil War, the wrong that Lincoln initially sought to correct. "My paramount object in this struggle *is* to save the Union, and is *not* either to save or to destroy slavery," Lincoln wrote in 1862, "If I could save the Union without freeing *any* slave I would do it, and if I could save it by freeing *all* the slaves I would do it; and if I could save it by freeing some and leaving others alone I would also do that." At that stage in the conflict, Lincoln seemed to believe his *post bellum* obligation was to restore the Union—restore its *mishpat*, its procedural rights—nothing else.[8]

Yet weeks later he issued the preliminary Emancipation Proclamation, eventually transforming the war into a crusade to crush

[8] See Eric Foner, *Fiery Trial: Abraham Lincoln and American Slavery* (New York: Norton, 2011), 228.

slavery. Years later, he and his allies in Congress permanently banned slavery through the Thirteenth Amendment to the Constitution, the acceptance of which Congress made a prerequisite for the defeated states to rejoin the Union. The war, or their understanding of the war, had changed.

Why did Lincoln pursue emancipation shortly after he wrote that destroying slavery was not his main aim? Perhaps Lincoln concluded that, in fact, he could not save the Union with slavery intact. Emancipation was simply a practical military matter, seeking to seize and liberate one of the Confederacy's main resources (slave labor). Or perhaps Lincoln's understanding of what truly caused the war changed and deepened: secession was the trigger, but slavery was the underlying cause. If the Union had won the war in 1862, before emancipation, it would have defeated secession; but no one, then or now, would believe the war had resolved the deeper, underlying issues that brought the conflict about in the first place. In that sense, a war that left slavery in place would be *insufficiently* just, at best, if not outright unjust for having reinforced an unjust system of slavery.[9]

Conciliation

The case of the American Civil War helps illustrate the importance of conciliation, addressing the long-term conditions necessary to prevent conflict from reemerging. If the Union had won the war without destroying slavery, it would have failed to achieve conciliation and failed to address the root causes of the conflict. (It ended up

[9] For contrasting views on the moral quality of the Civil War, see Foner, *Fiery Trial*; see also Harry S. Stout, *Upon the Altar of the Nation: A Moral History of the Civil War* (New York: Penguin, 2007).

failing conciliation in another way, by abandoning Reconstruction after 1877 and allowing segregation and Jim Crow to take root. Through the war, the Union defeated slavery, not white supremacy.) Another way of defining conciliation is that, after war, all parties must seek more than the vindication of their rights; they must seek to restore right relationships and a right ordering to society. They must pursue *tzadeqah* because, without it, grievances leading to conflict will remain and the war will have been fought in vain.

This is the final aspect of *jus post bellum* and is likely the hardest to achieve. Indeed, it is impossible to fully achieve because perfect justice is not achievable in this fallen world. Earthly justice exists along a spectrum: we can pursue a maximalist vision of full justice but inevitably must compromise with reality and settle for a more minimal, achievable vision. Where exactly the lines of compromise lie is rarely clear in the moment.

Through World War I, the United States successfully vindicated its maritime rights. (Germany had engaged in "unrestricted" submarine warfare in the Atlantic in blatant violation of the laws of war, murdering hundreds of civilians at sea from 1915–1917.) But President Woodrow Wilson correctly understood there were deeper issues at stake and sought a broader vision of postwar peace contained in his Fourteen Points, which included a ban on secret treaties, free trade and open seas, gradual disarmament, and some territorial adjustments. Those were reasonable aspirations for a more just and peaceful postwar world.

But one clause in the Treaty of Versailles—or, at least, the way it was interpreted—undermined that vision. The clause insisted that Germany and its allies were solely responsible for the war's destruction and demanded billions of dollars in reparations paid to France, Belgium, and others. Germans called this the "war guilt" clause and felt it unfairly pinned the blame on them for a continental catastrophe. The clause and especially the reparations poisoned relations among the former belligerents and made conciliation impossible. Leaders spent the better part of the next decade arguing about who owed whom and how to make a broken, impoverished Germany pay.

World War I was the result of a century of nationalism, great power rivalry, and imperial maneuvering triggered ultimately by a newly unified, rising, aggressive Germany and the failure of Europe and the United States to come to terms with it. A just ending to the war would have, somehow, undermined nationalism while accepting the reality of German power and also forcing Germany to accept the rules of international behavior. Instead, the Allies blamed Germany and saddled the continent with an economically unworkable reparations scheme while American diplomats took a holiday from history. The Allies won the war and lost the peace. They failed to achieve conciliation, stumbling in the home stretch and turning what could have been a just peace into an unjust and ruinous seedbed for the next conflict.[10]

Diplomats took the lesson to heart at the end of the Second World War. The Allies occupied Germany, established a military government, and put Nazi leaders on trial, introducing a fuller measure of *mishpat* justice than after the First World War. At the same time, instead of saddling Germany with reparations and debt, the US gave it billions of dollars of aid through the Marshall Plan. Germany also adopted a democratic constitution, helped form the European Coal and Steel Community (a distant predecessor

[10] For an overview of American diplomacy in the aftermath of World War I, see chapters 10–14 in Robert Kagan, *The Ghost at the Feast: America and the Collapse of World Order, 1900–1941,* vol. 2 (New York: Vintage, 2024).

to today's European Union), and eventually joined NATO. The postwar settlement restored right relationships and helped build a rightly ordered European community of nations. It helped achieve a much fuller measure of conciliation and *tzadeqah*.

It is important to note how the Allies' insistence on regime change and the Nuremberg Trials—on firmer *misphat*—was the essential condition for the deeper and longer lasting conciliation and *tzadeqah* that followed. If the Nazi government had lost the war but somehow clung to power, there would have been no plausible path to restored relationships. This is an important consideration today when some want to jump directly to *tzadeqah* and forget the importance of rectifying past wrongs and holding leaders accountable for crimes of aggression and violence.

4

War in the Twenty-First Century

The Twenty-First-Century Context

Just war is characterized by just cause, right authority, and right intention at the outset; by discrimination and proportionality in how it is fought; and by justice, order, and conciliation in the aftermath. How do we apply these principles today? What does it look like to think rightly about war and conflict in our day? Just war reasoning is best practiced through a case study approach, by looking at the specific details of real historical conflicts. That means the first step to thinking well is to have some understanding of our contemporary world.

The twenty-first-century security environment is characterized by four distinct types of political violence. First—despite the hope that the end of the Cold War brought an end to traditional security concerns—large, powerful, hostile nation-states still threaten their neighbors and the world with old-fashioned territorial aggression. Russia invaded Georgia in 2008, annexed Crimea in 2014, and invaded the rest of Ukraine in 2022. China "invaded" the South China Sea by constructing artificial islands and military bases in violation of international law and a ruling of the Permanent Court of Arbitration—an act of aggression that threatens to escalate into a conventional naval war.

Second, a number of wars have become "frozen conflicts." These are wars in which the shooting stopped despite the parties never reaching a resolution. Such is the case with Russian-sponsored secessionist movements in Georgia, Azerbaijan, and Moldova; in the disputed region of Kashmir between India and Pakistan; between North and South Korea; and between China and Taiwan (dating to the Chinese Civil War that ended in 1949). Such wars might restart at any time. Diplomacy and commerce take place under the constant threat of imminent violence.

Third, civil wars between weak states and allied militias, tribes, and factions, on the one hand, and various insurgents, tribes, and other factions, on the other hand, grind along throughout Yemen, Syria, Libya, Somalia, Colombia, and a host of other fragile and failed states across Africa and Asia. Many of these wars have been ongoing at a low simmer for decades; they may appear to be over until another round of violence flares up and renews hostilities. The enduring weakness and incapacity of state institutions is another word for anarchy, a key precondition for these wars' longevity.

Fourth, amid such anarchy, non-state actors, including terrorists, drug traffickers, weapons traffickers, slavers, and organized criminal cartels collectively pose a threat to peace, justice, and order throughout the world. They exist in a state of war against human civilization, deliberately putting themselves beyond the pale by intentionally murdering civilians (in the case of terrorists) or by profiting from organized criminality of such a scale as to challenge a state's authority. Such enemies of civilization are rightly called barbarians. The on-again-off-again war between Israel and the terrorist organizations of Hamas and Hezbollah more closely resembles this kind of conflict than any other.

Sometimes the categories blur together, as when big states use small insurgencies, tribes, or factions as proxies in their contest for power and influence. Iran sponsors militias and terrorist groups across the Middle East. The US partners with allied tribes to combat ISIS and Iranian militias. Russia props up Bashar-al Assad, the dictator of Syria, in his civil war against Syrian rebels.

How do we wrap our heads around this panoply of violence? Is there a way to cut through the complexity and draw a simpler map that explains what forms of political violence are unjust and which (if any) are just?[1]

The Free World

One way of drawing a mental map of twenty-first-century geopolitics is by observing the basic orientation of the nations of the world toward or against the ideals of freedom and equality. This is not a perfect map—ideally our map would orient nations toward or against *justice*, not freedom. But all countries claim to embody

---

[1] For a longer treatment of the contemporary security environment, see chapter 3 in Paul D. Miller, *American Power and Liberal Order: A Conservative Internationalist Grand Strategy* (Washington, DC: Georgetown Univ. Press, 2016).

justice; it is a contested concept and hard to measure. It is far easier to measure freedom and treat it as a proxy for justice, as long as we keep in mind it is an imperfect proxy.

During the Cold War, American leaders often claimed that the US was the leader of the "free world." That was only partly true, as the United States included many unfree nations, such as Pakistan, in its anti-Soviet coalition. However, the point remained that the US-led alliance stood for an international order of comparatively greater freedom and equality within and among nations than the Soviet Union did. The free world was a culture of world order characterized by democracy, civil liberties, free markets, entrepreneurialism, the rule of law, peaceful adjudication of disputes, freedom of the seas, and cooperative security. Though not practiced perfectly, the principled vision was a direct consequence of America's self-understanding as a "city on a hill," an exemplar of liberty and equality for all the world.

The United States sought to foster an international order modeled on its own principles because it believed such principles were not uniquely American. As President Ronald Reagan said in 1982, "We must be staunch in our conviction that freedom is not the sole prerogative of a lucky few but the inalienable and universal right of all human beings."[2] Or as President Obama said in 2011, "All people yearn for certain things: the ability to speak your mind and have a say in how you are governed; confidence in the rule of law and the equal administration of justice; government that is transparent and does not steal from the people; the freedom to live as you choose. These are not just American ideas; they are human rights. And that

---

[2] Ronald Reagan, "Address to Members of the British Parliament," June 8, 1982, https://www.reaganlibrary.gov/archives/speech/address-members-british-parliament.

is why we will support them everywhere."[3] Both presidents gave expression to an unabashedly universal vision.

After the Cold War, scholars began calling world order characterized by these ideals the "liberal international order," a regrettably clunky phrase, and they wondered if such an order might become truly global. Francis Fukuyama famously announced the triumph of liberal democracy as the "end of history," by which he meant the end of meaningful ideological competition over the best form of political and economic organization.[4] With the very long perspective of human history, we can affirm that a world order characterized by freedom and equality is, by far, the best we have yet seen, though its present reality is often messy and imperfect. If we are looking for a very concise (if simplistic) mental map of geopolitics in the twenty-first century, we can do worse than to categorize nations, peoples, and movements as for or against the free world.

Today, the free world faces challenges from without and from within. From without, hostile powers seek to attack and overthrow the culture of a free world order. Russia and China have become increasingly explicit in their opposition to it while Iran and North Korea never pretended otherwise. Some scholars have called this a return of "great power rivalry,"[5] though in retrospect, it seems less a return than a reawakening to what is, in fact, a perennial challenge.

---

[3] Barack Obama, "Remarks by the President at Cairo University," June 4, 2009, https://obamawhitehouse.archives.gov/the-press-office/remarks-president-cairo-university-6-04-09.

[4] Francis Fukuyama, "The End of History?" *National Interest*, Summer 1989, 3–18, https://pages.ucsd.edu/~bslantchev/courses/pdf/Fukuyama%20-%20End%20of%20History.pdf.

[5] See Matthew Kroenig, *The Return of Great Power Rivalry: Democracy Versus Autocracy from the Ancient World to the US and China* (New York: Oxford Univ. Press, 2020).

Terrorists, drug traffickers, and the other non-state actors also pose a challenge, though far smaller than that posed by great powers.

There are also challenges to the free world from within, though this is a complicated point. The free world is challenged by its own failures—but also by the overreaction of critics who are convinced those failures are irredeemable. A wave of populist and nationalist movements emerged and gained popularity throughout the world over the past fifteen years in reaction to perceived flaws of what critics called "globalism." While often compromised by prejudice and conspiratorial thinking, the germ of truth in populist nationalism was that the free world includes free markets, which always create winners and losers, and that global capitalism often erodes local cultural particularity and national distinctiveness. Populist nationalism poses no viable, positive vision superior to the free world order; it is a cure worse than the disease. But that does not excuse the free world from addressing genuine concerns about its own record.

With the free world order as an intellectual map, we can walk through major conflicts around the world today. These are case studies to show how to assess the relative justice of each side, how to identify what is at stake, and how to weigh the tactics and novel technologies used in combat. I have chosen conflicts that are diverse in type, geography, combatants, causes, scale, and tactics; yet I have also focused on conflicts that are consequential, having regional if not global implications. The United States is not a direct belligerent in any of them (yet), but American policymakers have expressed strong interest in them, and the US is involved, in various ways, with all of them.[6]

---

[6] For a fuller discussion of the relationship between world order and classical liberalism, see chapter 1 in Miller, *American Power and Liberal Order*.

Great Power War: Russia and Ukraine

Historical Background

In 2014, Russia invaded Ukraine and annexed the Crimean Peninsula.[7] It sponsored rebel factions waging a low-key insurgency in the eastern region of Donbas for the next eight years. In 2022, Russia followed up with a much larger invasion to conquer the whole of the country and incorporate it into the Russian Federation. Russian President Vladimir Putin made five related claims about Ukraine and NATO to justify his war.

1. Ukraine is not a distinct cultural entity. "Ukrainian" is just a subcategory of "Russian" and, as such, belongs under the sovereignty of Russia.
2. Ukraine was never supposed to be an independent political entity. It was part of the Russian Federation, and its independence from the Soviet Union was a mistake.
3. The United States is waging an aggressive campaign of diplomatic isolation and military encirclement against Russia by expanding the NATO alliance in violation of promises American officials made to Russian leaders after the Cold War.
4. Ukraine's effort to join the NATO alliance, and the alliance's promise of future membership to Ukraine, amounted to an aggressive land-grab, an encroachment on Russian territory and a violation of Russian sovereignty.

---

[7] For background on the conflict, see Jonathan Masters, "Ukraine: Conflict at the Crossroads of Europe and Russia," Council on Foreign Relations (2023), https://www.cfr.org/backgrounder/ukraine-conflict-crossroads-europe-and-russia.

5. War was necessary and justified to reunify Ukraine with Russia, keep it out of NATO, and defend Russian sovereignty and Russian identity from NATO expansion.[8]

Jus ad Bellum

Putin's professed justifications for war are false. Some partisans on either side have gone to great lengths to argue for or against Putin's historical and cultural claims about Ukrainian and Russian identity. But those claims do not matter. Enforcing political unity is not just cause for war even if the states in question happen to be culturally similar. Cultural similarity does not require political unity. Ukraine is not obligated to subsume itself under the Russian Federation even if all of Putin's claims about Russian history and Ukrainian identity are true (which they are not).[9] The United

[8] "Read Putin's Speech and His Case for War in Ukraine," *New York Times*, February 24, 2022, https://www.nytimes.com/2022/02/24/world/europe/putin-ukraine-speech.html.

[9] In the ninth century, a state emerged from the city of Kiev that stretched northward to encompass much of what is today western Russia. Russian historians later named this state "Kievan Rus." Russian nationalists claim Kievan Rus was the birthplace of Russia's Slavic and Orthodox civilization, that modern Russia is the successor and inheritor of the Kievan Rus mantle, and that modern Russia should rightfully govern the territories of the former Kievan Rus. Later, the Russian Empire governed much of what later became Ukraine from the late seventeenth century until the dissolution of the Soviet Union in 1991. But contrary to the Russian nationalists' narrative, Kievan Rus was a multilingual and multinational polity, not a proto-Russian-nationalist regime. Ukraine has a distinct language, culture, and history; and Ukrainians fought (and lost) a war from 1917–1921 to assert their independence from Russia, demonstrating their longstanding distinction from Russia's political history. Finally, if the Russian nationalists are right that Kievan Rus is the template

States was not justified in trying to force Canada to become part of America in 1812 just because of their similar history, language, traditions, and religion.

Second, Ukraine has a distinct political identity. Ukraine's independence was universally recognized in 1991, including by the Russian Federation. The Russian government recognized Ukrainian independence for over thirty years without raising an objection or citing any of Putin's later complaints. Ukraine held uninterrupted membership in the United Nations as a sovereign state. Nothing changed in 2022 to rescind or compromise Ukraine's legitimate claim to independence. Ukraine's separate identity and political independence mean that it plainly has just cause to defend itself and right authority to do so.

Third, Putin's claims about NATO are also false—or, at least, they do not justify war in response. Some American officials may have given private, nonbinding assurances to Russian president Boris Yeltsin in the early 1990s that the US would not seek to expand NATO. Those assurances were never formally expressed or codified in public statements, much less a binding treaty.[10] US officials in the early 1990s had no authority to preemptively veto any future application from potential member states, nor to prevent the North Atlantic Council from considering such applications, nor to bind future US presidents with private assurances. Officials could, at most, vote no when such applications came to the Council but, again, were not bound to do so.

---

for today, that would give title for Ukraine to conquer Russia, not the other way around.

[10] Mary Elise Sarotte, "A Broken Promise?" *Foreign Affairs* (September/October 2014), https://www.foreignaffairs.com/articles/russia-fsu/2014-08-11/broken-promise.

NATO's expansion was defensive, not offensive. Eastern European states, having just escaped from eighty years of Soviet imperial occupation, were understandably eager to seek security guarantees against renewed Russian aggression—which Putin subsequently proved was a rational fear. Putin claimed that NATO's expansion threatened Russian security, but his exaggerated threat perceptions do not give him a heckler's veto over European defense policy. Eastern Europeans also felt threatened and also had a right to seek security, which means that they had every right to apply for NATO membership and that NATO had every right to respond in kind.

Finally, even if we assume Putin's claims about American promises are true, they still do not justify war as a response. If the US gave a binding promise never to expand NATO through a ratified treaty, and subsequently withdrew from the treaty and broke its promise, that would understandably alarm and upset Russia, and Russia would be entitled not to trust America's word and to take precautions for its defense—yet it *still* would not justify a preemptive and aggressive war against Ukraine in response. Putin's behavior amounts to punching someone in the face then blaming the victim because "look at what you made me do." Nothing the victim did, short of throwing the first punch, would have "made" Putin invade Ukraine in the first place.

Proportionality and Great Power War

That Ukraine has just cause and right authority to wage a war of self-defense is morally straightforward. But there are more complex questions about how the war is waged, by whom, and toward what vision of postwar peace. In short, the war is not simply between Ukraine and Russia. The United States, the NATO alliance, and other nations have supported Ukraine by giving it weapons, training, and intelligence. Legally, those nations are not belligerents, and there are no allied ground troops inside Ukraine directly participating in hostilities against Russia. But those nations are very much part of the war. That carries dangers of escalation, which alters the moral calculus of the war's progress, purpose, and ending.

Every act that Ukraine and its allies take during the war must consider the possibility that it could provoke Russian escalation, expand the war, draw in the allies, or even become global nuclear war. That is a main reason the US and the allies have so strongly insisted on a limit to their involvement: no one wants the Russia-Ukraine war to become World War III. That is prudent strategy, but it is also born of an appreciation for the proportionality of the war and the kind of peace we seek in the aftermath. As much as Putin's invasion is wrong and as much as it threatens the foundations of world order, the US should not risk nuclear war for Ukrainian independence. That would be disproportionate; there are no scenarios in which that would yield greater peace and justice. As Ronald Reagan and Mikhail Gorbachev agreed at their summit in Geneva in 1985, "Nuclear war cannot be won and should never be fought."[11]

To fully weigh the moral quality of Ukraine's war and, especially, of NATO's assistance, we must recognize that this war is one step away from becoming another kind of war altogether. Total war, great power war, nuclear war, world war—these are all names for a kind of war that is so vast, so all-encompassing, so destructive that

---

[11] "Joint Soviet-United States Statement on the Summit Meeting in Geneva," November 21, 1985, Ronald Reagan Presidential Library and Museum, https://www.reaganlibrary.gov/archives/speech/joint-soviet-united-states-statement-summit-meeting-geneva.

it is qualitatively different from most other wars. Most wars are fought for smaller stakes. They are limited in their means. They are limited in scope, scale, weaponry, and geographic extent. The big wars strain against limits. The stakes are existential: the victor becomes the leading power of the world while the vanquished may disappear forever or be forever changed. The larger stakes mean fewer restrictions on the weapons and tactics of war. The big wars are notable for their brutality.

Big wars are not necessarily unjust, though violations of justice may be more common on all sides. But, recalling the importance of military necessity, we should insist that wars become total only if necessity demands it. That is why the United States and its NATO allies are right to refrain from directly intervening in the conflict. To do so would run an unacceptable and *unnecessary* risk of provoking a total war in a war that, so far, can and should remain limited. The destruction and killing of total war are so vast and the damage is so lasting that we should do everything possible to keep wars limited in scale and scope as long as possible.

There is a tragic aspect to this. If Russia had invaded a NATO member—Latvia, for example—the US should and would go to war to defend its independence and sovereignty. Under the terms of the NATO treaty, an attack on one member is considered an attack on all. The US would treat an attack on Latvia or Germany as an attack on New York or Virginia. That is exactly why Russia will *not* attack a NATO ally and exactly why Ukraine and others want NATO membership. NATO is a clear and effective deterrent. It makes sense from an American perspective. It is a way for us to communicate in advance that this is the line we will defend. We will not wait for aggressors to directly threaten American territory. We understand our security is inextricably entwined with European security (and East Asian security, through our alliances with Japan and others). But Ukraine is not yet a member of NATO. NATO is not obligated to defend Ukraine. If the US exceeded its obligation and chose to go to war anyway, the burden is on the United States for expanding the war, likely provoking nuclear war among the great powers.

Jus post Bellum

If justice were to prevail in Ukraine, Russia would cease military operations, withdraw from the country, return Crimea and Donbas to Ukrainian control, publicly apologize, and provide reparations to Ukraine—and Vladimir Putin would resign the Russian presidency and turn himself in for a war crimes trial. Absent divine intervention, that will not happen. What, then, can we hope and pray for? What would a just end to the Russo-Ukrainian War look like?

For a war to be just, it must result in lasting conditions of justice and peace in the aftermath—even if flawed and fallible, as all orders of justice and peace are in this fallen world. Russia cannot achieve justice in the aftermath of an unjust invasion, and whatever peace might befall Ukraine in the wake of a Russian conquest would be the peace of tyranny. As Tacitus said of the Romans, so too the Russians might succeed in creating a desert and calling it peace. There is no justice in a Russian victory.

The harder question is for the Ukrainians and the international backers who are providing it with weapons and moral support and waging economic war on Russia through sanctions. What kind of justice or peace can we achieve? Is any achievable? Do we have any reasonable chance of success?

That depends on the course of the war, and it is hard to say in advance what might happen. But we can think through some scenarios. In the first scenario, keeping in mind the obligation to pursue order, justice, and conciliation, Ukraine might achieve order by defeating the Russian military and some degree of justice by beginning the long process of reconstruction. If Ukraine wins a definitive victory and regains all its lost territory, the international community should be prepared to mount an ambitious reconstruction campaign and also admit Ukraine into NATO and the EU. Conciliation would depend on developments inside Russia.

The second scenario: short of outright victory, if sanctions hurt hard enough and the Ukrainian military holds out long enough, Putin may decide to shorten the war and only hold on to small portions of eastern Ukraine and Crimea and pull back from the rest. He will have proven his point about his ability to hold Ukraine hostage—indeed, hold European security hostage—and could likely count on the Ukrainian government being effectively cowed into submission for the foreseeable future. Ukraine will return to some modicum of order, but not to justice.

In that case, lasting peace may require Kiev and its international backers to agree to some kind of permanent neutrality, as Finland and Austria agreed to after World War II. Neutrality would allow something like normal life to continue in Ukraine and reduce the likelihood of renewed fighting. It would also enable economic life to resume, along with international aid, investment, and development, helping Ukraine escape the trap of state failure and frozen conflicts.

A third scenario: Russia gets bogged down in an intractable insurgency. The war drags on for years and destroys much of Ukrainian infrastructure and civic life, yet in the end the Russians are forced to withdraw, much as they were from Afghanistan in 1989. In that case, Ukraine would be whole, free, and seemingly at peace. It would also be shattered, impoverished, and dangerously prone to civil war between its pro-western half (west of the Dnieper) and its Russian-speaking population (primarily on the east side). In this scenario, Ukraine might achieve a long-delayed order, but justice and peace would require a much larger, longer, and more expensive international effort to bring Ukraine back into the family of nations. It would require billions in reconstruction and stabilization assistance, and possibly a UN monitoring mission to ensure Russia stays out and Ukrainians stay together.

In any scenario, the hardest part of the question is how the world should relate to Russia after the war. Just war requires justice and peace for all combatants, not just the victor or the victim. How do we work toward conciliation with Russia when its government has been guilty of one of the most flagrant, dangerous, and lethal acts of international aggression in generations?

That will, again, depend on the manner of the war's end and the Russian government's behavior. Assuming Putin retains power and remains unrepentant, it is likely the United States and its allies will have to move toward something like the Cold War policy of containment. Keep sanctions in place, move to isolate and cut off Russia from the resources of the developed world, and work patiently—and peacefully, as far as possible—to limit and push back on Russian influence throughout the world. It will be a generational effort. Containment is what you do when you have established the conditions for conciliation yet the other party refuses to meet them. Conciliation is a two-way process, and if the other party will not do its part, our obligation is to protect ourselves and steadily maintain order and as much justice as possible in the meantime.

If Putin loses power—as Soviet leaders did in the aftermath of their defeat in Afghanistan in 1989—then the world has both greater opportunity and greater responsibility. The last time Russia went through a regime change, the world squandered the opportunity to help Russia transition to a more just, transparent, accountable regime. Instead, Russia spent the 1990s deteriorating into a corrupt oligarchy, and the 2000s turning into a restored, rearmed, authoritarian great power implacably opposed to the free world.

We should not aim at violent regime change in Russia—the risks of provoking a nuclear power are too great. But if Putin brings himself down through folly and overstretch—and sporadic antiwar protests across Russia suggest Putin's grip on power is not as solid as he wants the world to believe—we will face one of the best opportunities in thirty-five years to help a great power move—at last—toward greater justice and peace. It would be a Herculean undertaking, but to fail again would invite catastrophe.

Frozen Conflicts: China and Taiwan

Historical Background

Communist and nationalist forces fought a long civil war in China from 1927 to 1949.[12] The nationalist forces had been a wartime ally of the US against Japan during World War II. The nationalist government was treated as one of the five victorious powers after the war, and they were given one of the five permanent seats on the UN Security Council. The communists, however, won the civil war and established the People's Republic of China (PRC). Nationalist

[12] For background to the conflict, see Lindsay Maizland, "Why China-Taiwan Relations Are So Tense," Council on Foreign Relations (2024), https://www.cfr.org/backgrounder/china-taiwan-relations-tension-us-policy-biden.

forces, calling themselves the Republic of China (ROC), fled to the island of Taiwan. Both claimed to be the sole government of all China, though in practice the PRC governed the mainland while the nationalists governed Taiwan.

The United States and the PRC fought on opposite sides of the Korean War (1950–1953) and continued to view each other with suspicion and enmity for years after. The US and much of the world recognized Taiwan, not the PRC, as the government of China from 1949 until the 1970s when President Richard Nixon began a rapprochement with the PRC as part of his Cold War strategy. Following Nixon's overtures, the US formally switched recognition from Taiwan to the PRC in 1979. Most of the world followed suit in ensuing years. (In 1971 the United Nations switched recognition and gave China's seat on the UN Security Council to the PRC.)

At the same time, the United States publicly committed to a policy of "One China, Two Systems" and together with Taiwan insists that the resolution of the dispute between China and Taiwan be resolved peacefully. The US Congress passed the Taiwan Relations Act which obligates the United States to provide for Taiwan's defense (to soften the blow of abrogating a 1955 mutual defense treaty). The US has sold billions of dollars of weaponry to the island over the past forty years. US officials used to adhere to a policy of "strategic ambiguity," refusing to say how far the US would go to defend Taiwan against Chinese attack, but recently have become more strident and explicit saying the US would indeed defend the island. In 2003, the US Congress mandated that Taiwan be treated as a "major non-NATO ally." Taiwan also produces a significant portion of the world's semiconductors necessary for computers (and many weapons systems), highlighting its strategic importance to the US and world economy.

Legally, Taiwan is not a sovereign nation; practically, it has been independent for over seventy years. Legally, the US is not treaty-bound to defend Taiwan in case of a Chinese attack; practically, it would seem a betrayal of decades of partnership not to. On top of these realities, China is a totalitarian autocracy that perpetrates genocide against the Uighurs in western China, does not respect freedom of religion or speech, and regularly violates international trade and sea law. Meanwhile, Taiwan gradually transitioned to a free-market democracy and respects the full range of human rights and civil liberties. Earlier, China had promised to respect Hong Kong's freedom when it retook control of the city from the British in 1997, a test for how China might treat a reunited Taiwan. China broke its promise and ended Hong Kong's democracy in 2020, undermining any assurances it might give today about respecting Taiwan's democratic nature.

Both China and Taiwan avow that "there is but one China, and Taiwan is part of China"—but neither side acts like it. They maintain a legal fiction about a single unified China while the facts on the ground tell a different story. Taiwan insists the dispute be resolved peacefully, but the PRC says that it reserves the right to use force to reclaim its "lost territory." Under these circumstances, does China have just cause to forcibly reunify Taiwan with the mainland—a just war to recover lost or stolen property, as just war tradition has long affirmed—or does Taiwan have the right of self-defense to resist reunification? Is the United States obligated to defend Taiwan, or would that amount to interference in another state's sovereign affairs?

The just war categories do not provide an automatic answer to these questions because the question of who has right authority and who has just cause is the very heart of the dispute between China and Taiwan.

Jus ad Bellum and Right Authority

Who has right authority, the PRC or Taiwan? Who is the legitimate ruler of Taiwan? China's claim to Taiwan is, like Russia's claim to Ukraine, based on shared cultural ties and on contestable historical claims. The island is mostly populated by Mandarin-speaking Han Chinese, which China believes gives it the right to rule the island. Like Putin's claims about Russian and Ukrainian identity, China's cultural claims do not matter. Enforcing political unity among culturally similar states is not a just cause for war. China has no right to enforce reunification just because China and Taiwan share a common culture, ethnicity, and language.

The historical and legal case is more complicated, but ultimately it also does not support the PRC's claims. Under its imperial dynasty, China ruled Taiwan for about two centuries (1683–1895). The imperial government then ceded Taiwan to Japan following defeat in war. (International law generally recognizes the legitimacy of territorial changes agreed upon and codified in treaties at the conclusion of wars.) The imperial government fell in 1911, supplanted by the nationalist government—which was soon embroiled in civil war against the communists. The civil war overlapped with the chaos of World War II, at the end of which the nationalists took control of Taiwan following Japan's defeat.

From 1895 to 1945, China did not govern Taiwan or own the island. In 1945, the nationalist government was, briefly, the internationally-recognized government of mainland China, and had also retaken control of Taiwan—but, practically speaking, by that late point in the civil war the nationalists did not control the mainland, while the communists never controlled Taiwan. Neither party controlled both; there never was a Chinese government that governed both mainland and island after 1895. The PRC's claim to

Taiwan rests on recognizing the legitimacy of the nationalist government, which controlled Taiwan in 1945—while also fighting a civil war against them because of their supposedly illegitimacy. When the communists took control of China in 1949, Taiwan was not part of it. While it is true that a previous Chinese government ruled Taiwan for a time, the PRC never did.

If someone buys (or steals) a house, they do not automatically have title to an adjacent parcel of land just because the previous owner used to own it a half-century ago—nor even if the previous owner buys back that parcel in the process of moving out of the house. On top of that, if the new homeowner is a clear and present danger to the neighborhood—if he is abusive to his own family, routinely bullies the neighbors, drives recklessly, ignores traffic laws, and cheats the local grocer every time he goes shopping—we would rightly be cautious about letting him get his hands on more land and resources *even if* he had legitimate title to it. China's irresponsible, unjust, and dangerous international behavior has brought it very close to abrogating its international rights, in which case it has even less to stand on in its dispute with Taiwan. In these circumstances, the PRC does not have just cause to launch a war of reunification with Taiwan, while Taiwan would have the right of self-defense if attacked.

Intervention, Proportionality, and *Jus post Bellum*

Taiwan has a right to defend itself because it is, in every respect except legal technicalities, independent. Is the United States permitted—or even obligated—to come to Taiwan's defense? If Taiwan has the right to self-defense, it has the right to seek assistance. It would be *permissible* for the US, or any other ally, to aid Taiwan in case of attack. That does not mean the US is *obligated* to help, nor that it would be prudent to do so. The answer here is very similar to the discussion above about American intervention in the Russian war in Ukraine. Ukraine and Taiwan have the right to defend themselves, but the risks of escalation and global war mean that the United States should be cautious about how aggressively to intervene.

The question is, Is it possible to fight a limited war against a nuclear power that does not escalate into general, global, nuclear war? Could the US fight a war against China in defense of Taiwan that does not escalate uncontrollably? We cannot know the answer, of course, so perhaps we should reframe the question: What are the risks and costs of trying to fight a limited war, compared to the risks and costs of *not* fighting it? The risk of fighting is that it could escalate and cause incalculable harm to the world through massive loss of life and damage to the global economy and the global environment.

The risk of not fighting is not as obvious, but it is still very real. There are differences between Taiwan and Ukraine that, I think, should prompt US policymakers to be more willing to take risks with China than with Russia. One difference is between having promised Ukraine future membership in NATO and having already signed a mutual defense treaty with Taiwan (in 1955) and designated it a "major non-NATO ally" (in 1980). Though the US abrogated the earlier treaty, the tie between the US and Taiwan is far stronger, deeper, and older than the ties between the US and Ukraine.

The second difference is that China is far more influential and important to the shape of the future world order than Russia. If the US adopted a policy of refusing to fight China to defend Taiwan, and China knew it, sooner or later the PRC would conquer the island. That would be, of course, devastating to the Taiwanese people. But beyond the loss of Taiwanese lives, freedom, prosperity, and dignity, the entire world loses something important: the precedent that territorial conquest is unacceptable. Remarkably, nations have refrained from wars of conquest and annexation since 1945—until Russia's annexation of Crimea in 2014. We live in a novel and wonderful stretch of geopolitical stability nearly unparalleled in history. (Instead, territorial changes since 1945 largely happened through civil wars and insurgencies fragmenting states.)

The culture of world order that ostracized the very idea of conquest and annexation is fragile and, thanks to Russia, nearly broken. Should China—an economic superpower, far larger than Russia, and rising in wealth and power—follow in Russia's footsteps, world order would be irretrievably lost. To many readers, this may sound abstract and hypothetical, the harms too distant and conjectural. That is because most Americans are—and I simply cannot stress this enough—extremely historically ignorant, complacent with the world they grew up in, unaware of how commonplace it was for the world to be otherwise, and provincial in their expectation that the world will continue being the way it has been throughout their lives up until now. A character in Ernest Hemingway's *The Sun Also Rises* quips that he went bankrupt gradually and then suddenly.[13] World orders collapse the same way.[14] The loss of Taiwan would likely be the tipping point that suddenly plunges the world into a chaotic and deadly new era.

A greater appreciation for history helps one understand how the world can change suddenly, and often for the worse; how often history takes unexpected, dramatic turns; and how rare and unprecedented the present moment in history has been. Most of history is, as Thomas Hobbes said, "a war of every man against every

---

[13] Ernest Hemingway, *The Sun Also Rises* (New York: Grosset & Dunlap, 1926), 141.

[14] I owe this idea to Bob Kagan, who made the Hemingway bankruptcy comparison in a talk some years ago.

man" in which human life is "solitary, poor, nasty, brutish, and short."[15] Our era of relatively greater freedom and prosperity is an aberration, not the norm. It does not take a large jump of imagination to understand that if the geopolitical clock were rewound to 1939—if dictators and tyrants invaded, conquered, and annexed at will with little to no consequence—our era would come to a rapid close.

After the French surrendered to Hitler in June 1940, the Nazis seemed invincible, having conquered all Western Europe in six months, and the British military seemed hopelessly overmatched. Winston Churchill sought to remind his fellow citizens what was at stake. It was not simply British sovereignty, or even European freedom, that was on the line in the coming Battle of Britain. "If we can stand up to him, all Europe may be free and the life of the world may move forward into broad, sunlit uplands," he said, "But if we fail, then the whole world, including the United States, including all that we have known and cared for, will sink into the abyss of a new Dark Age made more sinister, and perhaps more protracted, by the lights of perverted science."[16]

Churchill's warning is a description of what may unfold if our present era comes to an end. A new Dark Age: a world order run by totalitarians in Moscow and Beijing, empowered by the "perverted science" of nuclear weapons, cyber power, and artificial intelligence, with no prospects for human freedom or human dignity anywhere on the horizon, anywhere in the world, indefinitely.

That is the risk we run if we choose not to fight.

---

[15] Thomas Hobbes, *Leviathan*, ed. Edwin Curley (Indianapolis: Hackett, 1994), 76.

[16] Winston Churchill, "Their Finest Hour," June 18, 1940, https://winstonchurchill.org/resources/speeches/1940-the-finest-hour/their-finest-hour/.

Israel and Hamas

Historical Background

In 1917, British Foreign Secretary Arthur Balfour publicly committed his government to providing a homeland in Palestine for Jews.[17] Palestine was, at the time, governed by the Ottoman Empire—which was, in turn, at war with Britain during World War I. Britain's promise to support Zionist aspirations for a Jewish homeland was a bit of wartime convenience, a way to stir up trouble behind Ottoman lines. The same logic had led Britain to provoke and support the Arab Revolt against the Ottomans in 1916.

Britain took control after the war, forming the Mandate of Palestine under the League of Nations. Jews took Britain's promise seriously. The Zionist idea had been in circulation for over a century and had coalesced into a coherent political movement and immigration campaign by the late nineteenth century, but it was relatively small. After the war, Jewish immigration into Palestine surged. That led to tensions with Palestinian Arabs, understandably wondering what the Zionist vision would mean for them. Rising Arab nationalism led Arabs to see Zionism as irreconcilable with their own aspirations for Arab self-rule.

In 1947, after decades of rising strife and violence, the United Nations voted to partition the Mandate of Palestine and create two sovereign states: Israel and Palestine. Israel accepted the partition—meaning that it accepted in principle that there would be a sovereign, independent Palestinian state—and declared independence. The Arab states rejected it and declared war on Israel.

---

[17] For a reasonably balanced account of the history, see Charles D. Smith, *Palestine and the Arab-Israeli Conflict*, 10th ed. (Bedford, NY: St. Martin's, 2020).

The Palestinians had no say. Israel won the war and, in the fighting, expanded its territory. Up to 700,000 Palestinian Arabs left or were forced from their homes during the war, what the Palestinians call the *Nakba,* or "the Catastrophe."

For the next twenty years, Egypt and Jordan took control of the West Bank and the Gaza Strip, land that had been envisioned as part of the new state of Palestine, and made no move to midwife Palestinian independence. In 1958, Syria sponsored the formation of Fatah, a militant Palestinian organization; in 1964, Egypt sponsored the formation of the Palestine Liberation Organization (PLO). Both groups denied Israel's right to exist and launched a campaign of sporadic terrorism against Israel. In 1967, in the aftermath of another war against neighboring Arab states, Israel seized and occupied the West Bank and Gaza. Israeli settlers began to move into the territories.

In 1987, a series of protests and riots broke out by Palestinians against Israeli military occupation. Amidst the uprising—called the *intifada*—a more militant movement emerged called Hamas. Where the PLO and Fatah were driven by secular Arab nationalism, Hamas was devoted to the Islamist and jihadist ideals associated with the Muslim Brotherhood and, later, al-Qaida and other terrorist groups.

In 1993 and 1995, Israel and the PLO signed a series of agreements called the Oslo Accords, which recognized the newly created Palestinian Authority (PA) as the sole, legitimate representative of the Palestinian people. Israel committed to gradually handing over control of the West Bank to the PA. The PA (largely controlled by the PLO) recognized Israel's existence. The PA/PLO officially foreswore violence and committed itself to diplomacy to achieve Palestinian independence, a significant step in the PLO's evolution. Hamas denounced the Oslo Accords and never evolved.

The Oslo Accords envisioned a diplomatic process to resolve borders, security arrangements, Israeli settlements, the status of Jerusalem, and the Palestinian claim to their "right of return" to the homes they had left in 1947 and 1948. But Hamas refused to cooperate with the Oslo process, continued to deny Israel's right to exist, and did not foreswear violence. Israel ended its military occupation of the Gaza Strip in 2005, but otherwise the peace process saw little progress over the thirty years following the 1995 Oslo signing—in part because Palestinians elected a majority of Hamas representatives to their legislature. Hamas fought a short civil war against other Palestinian factions in 2006, was ousted from the West Bank, but took full control of Gaza. In 2023, after almost twenty years of sporadic violence between Israel and Hamas, Hamas launched a terrorist attack on Israel that killed up to 1,200 Israelis. Israel responded by invading Gaza with the intent of eradicating the terrorist group and reimposing its control over the Palestinian enclave.

Jus ad Bellum in 2023

The moral dimension of the immediate crisis is clear-cut and simple. Hamas is a terrorist organization that deliberately murders civilians and says it wants to destroy Israel. On the other side, Israel has a right to defend itself.

Some readers, and many of my students, feel sympathy for the Palestinians' cause. I share their sympathy, and I note that the best way to stand with the Palestinians is to support Israel's war to destroy Hamas. Hamas, a terrorist group devoted to the destruction of Israel, is the Palestinians' greatest enemy. The State of Palestine would likely have come into full existence long ago if Hamas (and Hezbollah) never existed. If you want to stand with the Palestinians, stand with Israel.

No morally serious discussion of the Israel-Hamas war can start without the premise that Israel and Palestine both have a right to exist as separate, sovereign states of equal legitimacy. That was the premise of the United Nations' 1947 partition plan and the 1995 Oslo Accords. Israel and Palestine disagree about their borders and security arrangements, but the basic principle of mutual recognition is the bedrock of any plausible, lasting peace.[18]

Hamas rejects both Israel's existence and the Palestinian Authority's legitimacy. Hamas fought a war against the Palestinian Authority, seized military control over the Gaza Strip, and set up an authoritarian government there. Hamas does not respect the human rights of its own Palestinian population, let alone of neighboring Israelis. According to Amnesty International—hardly an Israeli apologist—Palestinian authorities "unduly restrict freedom of expression, association and assembly, at times using excessive force to disperse peaceful gatherings." They singled out Hamas's government in Gaza for "a general climate of repression, following a brutal crackdown on peaceful protests."[19]

Israel and the Palestinian Authority recognize each other's existence within the territory of the former British Mandate of Palestine, but Hamas is a spoiler. Today, 165 nations recognize Israel as a legitimate sovereign state; 139 recognize the Palestinian

---

[18] Some Christians believe Israel has exclusive right to the entire land on the grounds of God's promises to Abraham in Genesis 12, 15, and 17. Against that view, I follow those who understand Rom 9:8 to mean that God's promises to Abraham are fulfilled through Jesus in the church and will be fully realized in the new creation, not in the modern state of Israel. I affirm modern Israel's right to exist on the basis of self-determination, international law, and humanitarianism, not biblical precedent.

[19] Amnesty International, "Palestine," https://www.amnesty.org/en/location/middle-east-and-north-africa/palestine-state-of/report-palestine-state-of/.

Authority as the sovereign government of Palestine. Yet Hamas thinks it knows better.

Some who sympathize with the Palestinians seem eager to downplay or excuse Hamas's terrorism done in the Palestinians' name. That is a gross mistake and a political miscalculation. Palestinian sovereignty does not justify terrorism. Terrorism delegitimizes the Palestinian cause and makes it very difficult to advocate for the Palestinians without becoming complicit with terrorism. Hamas is in the wrong *no matter what you think of the Palestinians' cause.* If you sympathize with the Palestinians, you should hate Hamas. Hamas hijacked the cause of Palestinian independence for its jihadist ideology and made it essentially impossible to support Gaza without being complicit with terrorism.

Hamas claims that Israel's very existence is a form of imperial occupation, that there should be no Israel at all, and that Palestine should own the totality of the former British Mandate of Palestine. Some parts of the American campus left clearly sympathize with this view, as evidenced by rallies and protests in favor of Hamas in the fall and winter of 2023. Such protesters need to understand that their view is not shared by the Palestinian National Authority, the United Nations, or the overwhelming majority of all countries and humans on earth.

On the other hand, their view is shared by Hamas, al-Qaida, Hezbollah, and Iran. Hamas itself openly states its goal: the complete destruction and eradication of Israel and the rejection of any negotiated settlement to the territorial dispute between Israel and Palestine.[20] That is an open avowal of genocidal intent. Hamas

---

[20] Bruce Hoffman, "Understanding Hamas's Genocidal Intent," *Atlantic*, October 10, 2023, https://www.theatlantic.com/international/archive/2023/10/hamas-covenant-israel-attack-war-genocide/675602.

intends to carry out ethnic cleansing until there are no Jews anywhere in the territory of what is today Israel and Palestine together. Hamas aims to grant Hitler a posthumous victory.

Jus ad Bellum before 2023

Set aside Hamas and its terrorist tactics. For the sake of argument, let us consider the broader case for a Palestinian war against Israel. Does Palestine have just cause? A just cause for war typically involves self-defense or the defense of peace, justice, and the common good against some kind of aggression.

Of what aggression was Israel guilty in 2023? Save the historical argument for a moment. In 2023, Israel did not occupy Gaza, having withdrawn in 2005; it had recognized the Palestinian Authority; and it had engaged in repeated negotiations to end the Israel-Palestine dispute. Israel did not initiate the recent round of violence in 2023. Under these conditions, Hamas is not fighting for self-defense, and political violence is not remotely a last resort for their cause. War must be a last resort, not an ongoing threat while on-again, off-again negotiations sputter along decade after decade while one side continues to vow the eradication of the other.

Only if you think that Israel's very existence is a standing aggression against the Palestinians can you conclude that the Palestinians have a right of war against them today. That is how Hamas could murder civilians in cold blood: they claimed that every Israeli is an "occupier" and thus a legitimate military target. Not even the UN, notorious for its rote condemnations of Israel, agrees with that sentiment. The UN voted in 1947 to create the state of Israel and the state of Palestine, affirming that the existence of one was consistent with the other. Israel's existence is not an aggression, and achieving

Palestinian statehood *at Israel's expense* does not constitute a just cause for war.

The strongest case that can be made for a Palestinian right of war is based on narrow and contested historical grounds: the *Nakba*. Just war theory has long affirmed that recovering stolen territory or property is a just cause for war. Does the *Nakba* qualify? That depends on our reading of history—and history on this subject is notoriously ambiguous. It is unclear the extent to which the Arab exodus was the result of Israeli compulsion and intimidation, how much was voluntary, and how much was encouraged by Arab leaders. The ambiguity undermines the Palestinian case for war, as war should be reserved for cases of clear-cut wrongdoing.

Just before the *Nakba*, something similar was happening a few thousand miles away in what became India and Pakistan. After the British drew a line of partition to create the Muslim state of Pakistan out of the largely Hindu subcontinent of India, tens of millions of people left their homes and relocated to the country where their religion predominated. The event was a bloodbath. Sectarian violence erupted across northern India as civilians massacred each other in an orgy of mutual ethnic cleansing.

The stories were similar across eastern Europe after World War II as borders were adjusted, refugees relocated, and random violence ruled ungoverned spaces in the wreckage of war. I am not suggesting with these comparisons that population movements in wartime are morally neutral, nor that we whitewash past wrongs. But if past events, especially those in the chaos of war and state failure, become the *causus belli* (reason for war) for another war, then every war will lead to the next, and there will never be peace, let alone justice. None of the events in India and Pakistan, or across Europe, have been cited as grounds for a future war by one party against the other.

Two final notes. First, even if we grant the historical argument—even if the Palestinians have a right of war because of the Arab exodus of 1948—it would be a war for compensation not independence, which is not at issue in the *Nakba*. Israel did not deny Palestinian independence in 1948—it accepted the partition plan—and the *Nakba* was not the reason Palestine failed to achieve independence. The Arab states' refusal to accept partition was the reason, in which case the Palestinians might have had a right of war against Egypt and Jordan, not Israel. But a war for compensation is clearly not the war that Hamas is waging against Israel today; Hamas is fighting a war to wipe Israel off the map, not regain homes in a limited slice of land lost in 1948.

Finally, since Israel recognized the PA in 1995 and committed itself to a peace process, war is not the Palestinians' last resort. They have a peaceful diplomatic channel to advocate for the "right of return" or for compensation. There is room for us to recognize ways in which Israel could work harder for justice and conciliation—Israeli settler policy is plainly unhelpful, and Israel probably should be open to some form of symbolic compensation—but the larger onus is on the Palestinians, whose regular disruptions of order through terrorism preclude any movement toward justice and conciliation. Just war should aim at a better peace. It is unclear how a Palestinian war against Israel would do that in Palestine, Israel, or the region. And whatever the wrongs of the past, they are not best solved through another war.

Jus in Bello

Israel's war against Hamas has been widely criticized on the grounds that it involves indiscriminate bombing, mass civilian causalities, the deliberate destruction of civilian infrastructure, and population displacement. In the aftermath of the attack on October 7, 2023, some Israeli officials said some alarming things that seemed to lend credence to these accusations. For example, Yoav Gallant, the Israeli defense minister, said, "We are fighting against human animals," as he announced a "complete siege" of Gaza, including by cutting off water and power.[21] In December 2023, South Africa brought a case before the International Court of Justice accusing Israel of committing genocide.

Set aside the overheated rhetoric for a moment to focus on the actual deeds of the Israeli Defense Forces (IDF). It is difficult to ascertain the truth of the allegations against them. To judge rightly, we would need full, unbiased, truthful information about (1) the IDF's targeting process and military deliberations and (2) where the bombs are falling and who is dying. Unfortunately, we do not have that information, at least not reliably. The IDF's spokesperson assures the world that Israel is doing all it can to avoid civilian casualties and is abiding by all the laws of war. But, of course, paid spokesmen will say what they are hired to say. As for where the bombs are falling and who is dying, most of the information coming out of Gaza is controlled by Hamas and repeated uncritically by international news media with a record of hostility to Israel. There is no reason to give Hamas's propaganda or its international sympathizers any credence. Both sides will spin events to their benefit, leaving us either credulous parrots of one side or the other, or

---

[21] Emanuel Fabian, "Defense Minister Announces 'Complete Siege' of Gaza," *Times of Israel*, October 9, 2023, https://www.timesofisrael.com/liveblog_entry/defense-minister-announces-complete-siege-of-gaza-no-power-food-or-fuel/. See also Yair Rosenberg, "What Did Top Israeli Officials Really Say about Gaza?" *Atlantic*, January 21, 2024, https://www.theatlantic.com/international/archive/2024/01/israel-south-africa-genocide-case-fake-quotes/677198/.

epistemological nihilists, comprehensive skeptics unable to make a judgment for want of good information.

We can avoid such total skepticism. Because Israel is a relatively open democracy, there exists accessible, verifiable information about it. Two scholars visited Israel in 2014 and 2015 to study the IDF's targeting practices. Their research included "unprecedented access that included a 'staff ride' of the Gaza area, inspection of an Israeli operations center responsible for overseeing combat operations, a visit to a Hamas infiltration tunnel, review of IDF doctrine and other targeting guidance, and briefings by IDF operators and legal personnel who have participated in targeting," as well as interviews with senior ISF officers and legal advisors. The scholars concluded that "IDF operations are clearly well-regulated and subject to the rule of law. The IDF has extremely robust systems of examination and investigation of operational incidents, and there is significant civilian oversight. . . . The extent to which [legal] officers are independent of commanders, especially when providing legal advice during ongoing operations, is striking."[22]

The authors expressed some concern that ground commanders did not have the same level of legal oversight that air commanders did, but they concluded overall that "there were no findings that would mark Israel as an outlier with respect to any particular norm." Some Israeli officials surely presented a Potemkin village to the scholars, but the depth and consistence of their access (they visited more than once) lends validity to their overall observations.[23]

---

[22] Michael N. Schmitt and John J. Merriam, "The Tyranny of Context: Israeli Targeting Practices in Legal Perspective," *University of Pennsylvania Journal of International Law* 37, no. 1 (2015): 53–139, quotations on 56, 136–37.

[23] Schmitt and Merriam, 138.

As recently as 2015, then, the IDF could not be credibly accused of "indiscriminate" targeting or intentional war crimes.

Now, in light of the horrific killings of October 7, 2023, and the rhetoric by some Israeli officials in the immediate aftermath, it is possible, even likely, that some individual Israeli soldiers and targeters felt they had permission to relax standards or that they gave in to anger and used excessive force. Additionally, Israel reportedly adopted a new automated system for identifying targets shortly after the war started. The AI-powered system, code-named "Lavender," enabled the Israeli military to identify and strike targets much faster—but with almost no human oversight and with much greater allowance for civilian casualties. "The [Israeli] army also decided during the first weeks of the war that, for every junior Hamas operative that Lavender marked, it was permissible to kill up to 15 or 20 civilians," according to the report on Israeli's new system. By contrast, "in the past, the military did not authorize any 'collateral damage' during assassinations of low-ranking militants."[24] The wide permissions granted to Lavender would be a striking departure from what the scholars observed in 2015.

If such reports prove true (the Israeli military denied them), they raise troubling questions about Israel's war. The choice to allow up to twenty civilian casualties for every low-level militant killed is a human choice, not a function of the AI targeting system. It does not constitute genocide, as Israel's harshest critics argue, but suggests that Israel has adopted a much laxer calculus about proportionality and discrimination. Whether this constitutes an unjust disproportionality depends in part on the time horizon

---

[24] Yuval Abraham, "'Lavender': The AI Machine Directing Israel's Bombing Spree in Gaza," *+972 Magazine*, April 3, 2024, https://www.972mag.com/lavender-ai-israeli-army-gaza/.

within which we assess Israel's choices. If seen only as retaliation for the attack of October 7, Israel's approach—which may have killed over 30,000 Palestinians so far—is surely disproportionate, if not callously negligent. In that light, Israel's record in the first weeks after October 7 and its use of Lavender and similar AI systems are hard to justify.

The best way to understand the Israeli military's shift in targeting and tolerance for civilian casualties is by placing it on a much longer time horizon: it is a response, not solely to October 7, but to a century-long campaign by its neighbors and enemies to deny its legitimacy and end its existence. But not even that exonerates Israel, which seems to be placing the burden for a century of wrongdoing on present-day Palestinian civilians who have little agency to undo the wrongs of the past. And that is before we even consider the ethical implications of Israel's handing over wartime decisions to an algorithm. (See chapter 5 for a discussion of the ethics of autonomous weapons and AI in warfare.)[25]

Nonetheless, we should also note that on the other side of the battlefield, a different picture emerges. By their own admission, Hamas openly practices indiscriminate war by deliberately targeting civilians. They claim, in fact, that there are no such things as Israeli civilians, that every Jewish man, woman, and child is an "occupier" and thus a legitimate target. They openly call for genocide. Hamas's militants engage in hostilities without wearing identifiable uniforms, they hide among a civilian population, and they use civilians as human shields. These are all war crimes, and Hamas openly and repeatedly commits them in clear, undisputed circumstances. These are uncontested facts; no one, including Hamas, claims otherwise.

---

[25] Abraham, "'Lavender.'"

There is no moral equivalence between Hamas's deliberate, open murder of civilians—which they do not deny and openly celebrate—and inadvertent civilian casualties—even a troublingly large number of them—from Israeli airstrikes or the excessive use of force by errant commanders and soldiers in the heat of the moment. The moral and legal responsibility for placing Palestinians in harm's way lies first and most heavily with Hamas. The Geneva Conventions are clear: if a combatant uses a school, hospital, or religious facility for a military purpose, it is no longer a protected civilian location. It is a legitimate military target. Hamas started the war with an act of grotesque terrorism on October 7 and could end it any time (the war is ongoing at the time of this writing) by surrendering and freeing its hostages. Hamas could further advance the cause of the Palestinian people by renouncing violence, revoking their charter, recognizing Israel, unilaterally disbanding, and handing power back to the Palestinian Authority.

Jus post Bellum

What is the justice that Israel's war against Hamas should achieve? The death or capture of Hamas's leadership is the precondition of justice, but not the exhaustive parameters of it. As the United States found in Iraq and Afghanistan, killing and capturing militants might create peace for a day, but militant groups can easily regroup unless and until underlying conditions are addressed. Israel should aim at more than the destruction of Hamas.

The war should be, in fact, an opportunity to revive or replace the Palestinian Authority, restart the peace process, and move toward an independent Palestine that recognizes Israel's existence. The Arab States' rejection of the 1947 partition plan was the original sin that deprived the Palestinian people of their independence and Israel of its right to live in security. Ever since, the Palestinians have been stateless, and Israel has lived under constant threat of war, terrorism, unrest, and international ostracism. There will be no lasting or just peace in Israel or Palestine until each recognizes the other and both can live free from the threat of daily violence. An independent Palestine would remove a key grievance that terrorists exploit for recruitment, and an independent *democratic* Palestine would give Palestinians an avenue of peaceful political participation.

Unfortunately, at the time of this writing, there is little evidence that Israel is thinking beyond Hamas's destruction. Prime Minister Benjamin Netanyahu suggested that Israel will reimpose a military occupation on Gaza after the war, and he rejected Palestinian statehood, reversing decades of Israeli policy. It is unclear how that would lead to lasting peace or security. Israel, in all likelihood, is falling into the trap Hamas laid for it. The point of Hamas's terrorist attack on October 7 was to draw Israel into an impossible situation, getting bogged down in urban warfare and military occupation that will make Israel look like the aggressor and the Palestinians the victims. Such a scenario, Hamas hopes, will isolate Israel on the world stage, starving them of support and resources. An isolated Israel is one that Hamas believes it can outlast, exhaust, and eventually eradicate.

Israel should, instead, define this as a war to liberate itself and Palestine alike from Hamas's tyranny. Justice demands that Israel live in security; it also demands that Palestinians live in dignity. Israel did not oppose the creation of a Palestinian state in 1947 and affirmed in 1995 its willingness to transfer sovereignty to the Palestinian Authority. The Oslo Accords showed that, as recently as the 1990s, there were parties on both sides willing to move toward that goal. Hamas (and Hezbollah) is the main obstacle to further progress, along with the PA's own corruption and incompetence.

That is another reason Israel's lax targeting practice and high tolerance for civilian casualties is troubling; it bespeaks little concern for justice and conciliation in the aftermath of the war, and little love for the Palestinians whose security and independence should be one of the fruits of a justly fought war.

It may sound counterintuitive to say that Israel's response to Hamas's terrorism should result in Palestinian independence. Some may even feel that Palestinian independence would be a victory for the terrorists' demands. So it is important to emphasize that terrorists do not demand an independent Palestine alongside a co-equal, independent Israel; they demand an independent Palestine and no Israel at all. Israel's war should kill, capture, or delegitimize the terrorists and sympathizers who still cling to that murderous vision. But we should not let that obscure the fact that an independent Palestine, alongside an independent Israel, was—again—the original vision of the UN partition plan, accepted by Israel, and supported by most of the world since the Oslo Accords. An independent Palestine is an important part of what justice demands in the Middle East.

5

Technological Advancements in Warfare

The Technology of Warfare

People can kill each other with any weapon imaginable. The Bible does not tell us what Cain used to kill Abel—just that he "attacked his brother Abel and killed him" (Gen 4:8)—but we can imagine he used one of his farm tools or Abel's shepherd's crook or a rock or even his bare hands. Samson famously killed the Philistines with a donkey's jawbone and, later, killed even more by collapsing a building on them. David killed Goliath with a slingshot and a stone, and Jesus used a whip to drive the money lenders from the temple. The prophet Jeremiah envisioned God using Israel (or possibly the Messiah) as his "war club . . . [his] weapons of war" to "smash nations" (Jer 51:20); and the prophet Isaiah warned against trusting in chariots and horses (Isa 31:1), the weapon of mass destruction of the ancient world.

Today we use pistols, rifles, shotguns, and machines guns. We use bombs, including those fired from tanks, airplanes, submarines, rockets, and battleships; but as the Rwandan genocide showed, machetes still do just as well. Bashar al-Assad used chemical weapons in his civil war almost exactly a century after their debut in World War I. Rifles are about 150 years old, building on the technology of the musket, which dates back a half-millennium from the blunderbuss to the arquebus. Gunpowder-based weapons go back even further: artillery dates to at least the fourteenth century, and gunpowder was used in some explosives and incendiary devices even earlier.

Before we shot and blew each other up, we had to content ourselves with stabbing, slashing, hacking, and smashing one another with hunks of metal, just as in biblical times. Swords and arrows, the paraphernalia of romantic adventure movies today, were the unromantic tools of order, murder, and warfare for unnumbered centuries: short swords, longswords, and broadswords; the Scottish claymore, Arabian scimitar, and Japanese katana; the duelist's rapier and sailor's cutlass and horseman's saber. Daggers, knives, lances, maces, axes, pikes, and spears—and that was just the infantry. The archers had their longbows and crossbows. The cavalry had their pick: Genghis Khan conquered nearly all Eurasia with stirrups and composite bows, the former to steady mounted warriors and the latter to let their arrows fly farther and faster. And then there are the siege engines, battering rams, catapults, and more.

Is there anything new that needs to be said about the morality of the technology of warfare? The ethics of conventional weapons has been exhaustively covered during the long millennia of their use. Three weapons stand out in the twenty-first century. First, nuclear weapons are not entirely new, but the ethics surrounding their use is complex and still merits consideration. Second and third, the most pressing need for ethical reflection is guidance for the newest of tools for killing—AI autonomous weapons—and for potentially lethal cyberwar.

Nuclear War

Most bomb technology works through the process of combustion. Set fire to gunpowder or TNT or certain kinds of plastic, and they combust with an enormous release of energy. Surround the explosive material with metal, and the explosive energy will shatter and propel bits of jagged metal outward. It is the jagged metal (shrapnel), not the explosion itself, that usually kills its victims. In a sense, most bombs are just thousands of tiny swords stabbing outward infinitely faster than any arm could thrust. The lethality of a bomb is limited to the blast radius of the explosion, which is limited by the amount of energy released. The ethical considerations of conventional bombs are thus limited by the physical limitations of combustion. The ethics are often circumscribed by the physics.

Nuclear weapons are different. They rely on a nuclear, not a chemical, reaction. The plutonium or uranium atoms that make up the nuclear core either split or fuse (depending on whether it is a fission or fusion bomb), which releases thousands or even millions of times more energy than combustion. Nuclear explosions kill people three ways: (1) through the resulting fireball, (2) the shock wave of compressed air that radiates outward at thousands of miles per hour, shredding cities and peoples with flying concrete and steel. But (3) the crucial difference from conventional explosives is that nuclear weapons also kill and maim over a longer time through radiation exposure, which is not limited to the blast radius.

Nuclear weapons have been almost universally condemned as immoral tools of warfare. Many Christian organizations expressed caution, even ire, at the use of nuclear weapons against Japan to end World War II. "Among the nation's clergy, an overwhelming majority responded to the atomic bombs with trepidation, fear, and moral outrage," and not just among pacifist or leftist denominations, according to Andrew Preston.[1] Years after the bombing, Carl F. H. Henry, writing in 1952, expressed unease about it and asked pointed questions about the US government's ability to use nuclear weapons ethically. "We are devoting the genius of our age to the development of weapons so destructive that they have no value for defense, but can serve only an offensive and destructive purpose," Henry wrote. In reference to Hiroshima, Henry argued that "they dropped the bomb, and if there was any guilt in the dropping of that bomb, in the sudden erasure of those Japanese lives, in the distorted features and ugly scars and suffering bodies which we bequeathed to a multitude of blistered survivors, we share in that guilt." Henry was concerned that the US had entered the era of nuclear war without adequate ethical consideration: "Our political and military leaders did so without preparing the inhabitants of our great land to think through the ethical implications of the use of the bomb, and as a consequence . . . there is the greatest moral uncertainty and indefiniteness in the minds of great masses of people about the ethical legitimacy or illegitimacy of such a weapon in modern warfare."[2]

---

[1] Andrew Preston, *Sword of the Spirit, Shield of Faith: Religion in American War and Diplomacy* (Canada: Knopf, 2012), Kindle loc. 8757.

[2] Quoted in Timothy Padgett, *Swords and Ploughshares: American Evangelicals on War* (Bellingham, WA: Lexham, 2018), Kindle loc. 2558ff.

The just war tradition teaches that war must be fought with discrimination and proportionality: we should not use excessive force, kill noncombatants, or use means out of proportion to the ends we seek to achieve. The argument against nuclear weapons is that they are, by their very nature, indiscriminate and disproportionate. Critics argue that (1) nuclear weapons are so big that they cannot be targeted solely at military targets and (2) they are so big that there is no conceivable aim for which their use could be the proportionate response. The US National Conference of Catholic Bishops captured this sentiment with their 1983 encyclical, *The Challenge of Peace*, which essentially condemned any possible use of nuclear weapons.

The argument against nuclear weapons is persuasive in many, even most, cases. It would be wrong, however, to assert *a priori* that it must always be true in every case. This is a situation in which we cannot make a sweeping statement on principle; we must examine the facts of nuclear weapons and the scenarios of their likely use. One relevant fact is that nuclear weapons come in a variety of sizes. To condemn all nuclear weapons based on their size overlooks the fact that some nuclear weapons are comparatively small (though still bigger than conventional explosives), while others are truly monstrous. The fifteen-kiloton bomb dropped on Hiroshima had a blast damage and thermal radiation radius of just over a mile. The largest nuclear weapon ever tested—the Soviet Union's fifty-megaton "Tzar Bomba"—had a blast and thermal radiation radius of nearly *forty miles*.[3] There is a significant difference between large and small nuclear weapons and how they can be used. Some nuclear bombs might be small enough to use discriminately, especially

[3] For different weapons' capabilities, see the online interactive tool "NukeMap," https://nuclearsecrecy.com/nukemap/.

because—another relevant fact—some types of targets (aircraft carriers, armored formations, underground bunkers, missile silos, etc.) are often removed from civilian populations. A small nuclear weapon against a large, hardened enemy formation or facility on a battlefield far removed from civilians would likely pass the test of discrimination.

What about proportionality? Wars, like bombs and targets, also come in different sizes. A nuclear weapon used in a low-stakes military operation—to kill a single terrorist or rescue a hostage or fight a drug cartel—would surely be disproportionate. But a nuclear weapon used to end World War II—a total war in which the very existence of whole nations and peoples was at stake—has a much stronger argument for being proportional to the cause.

I would add two qualifications to limit even a constrained use of nuclear weapons. First, my argument applies to smaller nuclear weapons used against military targets. During the Cold War, nuclear arsenals in Russia, the United States, and China mostly relied on much larger weapons targeted at enemy cities as a deterrent against attack: everyone threatened each other with annihilation as the ultimate form of protection. Some scholars defended such weapons as purely defensive and, in fact, a positive contribution to peace. This is the theory of "mutually assured destruction," which, they said, ensured that the great powers will never fight a total war ever again.[4]

While this theory has held true for the past eighty years, there is no guarantee it will continue to be true. Such a view places too much faith in decision-makers' rationality and goodness. And the

[4] Kenneth N. Waltz, "Nuclear Myths and Political Realities," *American Political Science Review* 84, no. 3 (1990): 731–45, https://doi.org/10.2307/1962764.

theory depends on threatening to do a thing—nuclear genocide—that would be, by any measure, wildly immoral to carry out. The existence of massive nuclear weapons deliberately targeted at civilian populations is indefensible. "Counter-population" nuclear war—and the theory of mutually-assured destruction that depends on it—has no possible moral justification, and the massive strategic nuclear weapons built for it are nothing but tools of genocide. (A more limited form of deterrence that aims, not at cities, but at rival nuclear forces, is more defensible.)[5]

The second qualifier has to do with radioactive fallout. Radiation and radioactive fallout from nuclear explosions, not their bigness, are the most troubling aspects of nuclear weapons. Radioactive fallout drifts on the wind. It cannot be targeted and lingers for years after wars end, which makes all nuclear weapons, to some degree, intrinsically indiscriminate. We cannot guarantee that radioactive fallout will only affect military targets. There are ways of minimizing radioactive fallout. A nuclear explosion set off in the air above a target—an airburst explosion—creates much less radioactive debris compared to weapons set off on the ground. Unfortunately, some of the likeliest targets for limited nuclear war—underground bunkers or enemy missile silos—require ground or close-to-ground bursts.

Nuclear weapons are not intrinsically immoral, but they are very difficult to use in an ethically justifiable way. Because they have greater potential for destruction and there is greater difficulty in using them discriminately and proportionately, policymakers must work much harder to constrain their use. Small nuclear weapons

---

[5] Paul Ramsey wrote extensively on the ethics of nuclear weapons and theories of deterrence. See Ramsey, *The Just War: Force and Political Responsibility* (Lanham, MD: Rowman & Littlefield, 2002); Ramsey, *War and the Christian Conscience* (Whitefish, MT: Literacy Licensing, 2011).

used against large, military targets above ground far removed from civilian centers seem to pass the test for justifiable use. Large nuclear weapons aimed at population centers are clearly immoral tools of genocide. In between are the harder cases: small or medium-sized weapons used against military targets in proximity with civilian centers, or used in a way that creates indiscriminate radioactive fallout. In those cases, policymakers are stuck with the same calculus as before: Is the likely harm to civilians outweighed by the stakes of the conflict? Are nuclear weapons the best and only tool for accomplishing what is militarily necessary? For most wars and most scenarios, the answer is likely no, but not always.

AI and Autonomous Weapons

One of the most enduring tropes of science fiction is the threat of killer robots, from HAL 9000 in *2001: A Space Odyssey* to the replicants in *Blade Runner*, the T-800 in *The Terminator*, and the AI in *The Matrix*. The fears are not new. In the 1940s, Isaac Asimov wrote a series of short stories about artificially intelligent robots. In his world, AI is governed by the "Three Laws": robots may not harm humans or, through inaction, allow a human to be harmed; they must obey orders from humans; and they must preserve their own existence—each law taking precedence over its successors.[6] Ever since we invented the computer, we seem to have had an instinctive, gut-level fear that the machines we create would become sentient, escape our control, and turn on us.

Our fears parallel our determination to build ever-more automated ways of killing each other. Autonomous weapons are not

[6] Isaac Asimov, *I, Robot* (New York: HarperVoyager, 2013).

new. In 1980, the United States Navy fielded the Phalanx Close-In Weapons System (CIWS), a network of automated, radar-guided guns designed to detect and shoot down enemy aircraft and missiles. Though supervised by humans, when active the system is designed to detect targets and fire autonomously. While the Phalanx is purely defensive, other autonomous systems can be used offensively. Mines are another kind of older autonomous weapon. Buried underground or placed on a seabed, mines automatically trigger and explode when they sense motion, heat, or pressure above.

These systems show that lethal automated weapons systems are already a reality, though still a far cry from the science fiction trope because the decision-making mechanisms, until recently, were still rudimentary. None of those systems were self-learning. Newer systems use advances in machine-learning and robotics to give weapons more autonomous movement and targeting. In 2013, Boston Dynamics, an AI and robotics firm, built Atlas, a bipedal, vaguely humanoid robot capable of autonomously performing mechanical tasks and demonstrating "athletic intelligence."[7] You have likely seen videos of the robot walking about, jumping on platforms, and carrying tools. In 2020, Boston Dynamics began selling Spot, an autonomous quadruped robot (modeled on a dog), as a potential helper for dangerous tasks (the Massachusetts State Police uses one on their bomb squad, for example). These are just a few of the autonomous vehicles, robots, and self-learning machines powered by AI software that have been under development for decades. Militaries can now employ a variety of autonomous systems as sensors and sentries for missile and air defense to help with explosives and ordnance removal and other tasks.

---

[7] See Boston Dynamics, https://bostondynamics.com/faq/.

Most controversially, some weapons systems have the ability to kill autonomously. Loitering munitions, for example, are armed, unmanned aerial vehicles programmed to hover over or circle a location, autonomously detect when a target is available, and fire. Drones and drone swarms can be given autonomous abilities (imagine a fleet of ten thousand small kamikaze drones surgically crashing into targets all over an enemy city). The same technology and decision-making software can be employed in a variety of platforms, including land-, sea-, and space-based vehicles armed with any sort of munition. Perhaps the T-800 is not so far off.[8]

Autonomous weapons could make war less lethal, more precise, and thus more just—if the data set on which the weapon is trained is consistent and accurate, if the decision-making software contains sufficient constraints on machines' autonomy, and if humans retain ultimate control over (and responsibility for) the machines' decision-making. Machines might, one day, become better than humans at discriminating between targets, aiming precisely, and using the minimum force necessary to achieve a goal. They cannot succumb to bloodlust or rage, will not commit war crimes out of malice or hatred, and will not rape or steal for profit, revenge, or dominance. Ironically, machines could make war more humane by taking the human out of war. "The real evils in war are love of violence, revengeful cruelty, fierce and implacable enmity, wild resistance, and the lust of power, and such like," Augustine wrote, "and it is generally to punish these things, when force is required to inflict the punishment, that, in obedience to God or some lawful authority, good men undertake

---

[8] See chapters 1–3 in Paul Scharre, *Army of None: Autonomous Weapons and the Future of War* (New York: Norton, 2018).

wars."[9] Robots are immune to the very things Augustine warned were the "real evils" of war.

Machines will, inevitably, make mistakes and kill the wrong person or select the wrong target. So do humans. The question is, Can machines be trained to make fewer mistakes than humans do? If the development of driverless cars is an indication—which shows promise but is taking longer than originally expected—the answer is probably yes, eventually; but it will take longer, and we should expect a long period of mistakes in the meantime. That means policymakers should keep AI weapons in development, off the real-life battlefield, for longer than they want, to ensure those weapons are as refined and ready for use as possible. The need for patience in deploying AI systems is widely recognized. In early 2023, several leaders in the tech industry published an open letter calling for a pause in research and development on artificial intelligence out of concern that the potential consequences were too great and too unpredictable while the governance and ethical norms on the use of AI were too underdeveloped. The tech leaders argued a pause was necessary to give time "to jointly develop and implement a set of shared safety protocols for advanced AI design and development that are rigorously audited and overseen by independent outside experts."[10]

---

[9] Augustine, "Against Faustus," bk. XXII, chap. 74, quoted in Arthur Holmes, *War and Christian Ethics* (Grand Rapids: Baker Academic, 2005), 64.

[10] "Pause Giant AI Experiments: An Open Letter," *Future of Life Institute*, March 22, 2023, https://futureoflife.org/open-letter/pause-giant-ai-experiments/. Sixteen AI companies agreed to a range of ethical guidelines at a global AI summit in South Korea in May 2024. See Joyce Lee, "Second Global AI Summit Secures Safety Commitments from Companies," Reuters, May 21, 2024, https://www.reuters.com/technology/global-ai-summit-seoul-aims-forge-new-regulatory-agreements-2024-05-21/.

Some scholars have raised a concern that allowing machines to decide when and whom to kill violates human dignity. "Shirking our responsibility to enact justice by passing it on to automated systems reveals a lack of concern for the human beings affected by our decisions in our desire for a quick ending to combat," Jason Thacker argues. "Using AI weapons, we do not come near to those we engage in combat and do not often think of them as men and women with families, livelihoods, hopes, and dreams. . . . AI can desensitize us to the reality that in war, real human lives are lost."[11] In Gen 9:6, God ordained, "Whoever sheds human blood, by humans his blood will be shed, for God made man in his own image." God delegated *to humans* the responsibility for bearing the sword against the evildoer. It is not clear that we, in turn, are permitted to delegate that responsibility to creations of our own.

I think this is true in an ultimate sense—we should never hand over complete control over warfare, national security, and public order to autonomous systems that run with no human oversight—but that does not mean all killing must take place face-to-face, in hand-to-hand combat, that we must look our enemies in the eye as we kill them. Impersonal killing is not a new or distinctive feature of AI weapons. Crossbows were maligned in their day as cowardly, dishonorable weapons compared to the courtly manliness of melee weapons and short-range archery, which demanded personal risk and intimate violence. Muskets and cannon, machine guns and tanks, were all subjected to the same critique that was ultimately little more than anachronistic chivalry. New weapons that bring a

---

[11] Jason Thacker, *The Age of AI: Artificial Intelligence and the Future of Humanity* (Grand Rapids: Zondervan, 2020), 134.

"quick ending to combat" (see previous paragraph) can be a good thing. There is no virtue in prolonging fighting and risking more lives just to make war more personal and chivalrous. "There is no legal, ethical, or historical tradition of combatants affording their enemies the right to die a dignified death in war," Paul Scharre notes.[12] Nor is dying from a machete or cannon somehow more humane or dignified than death by an algorithm. Dead is dead.

Perhaps the criticism has more to do with our heart attitudes when we engage in war. If so, again, impersonal combat may be a virtue because it protects us from "the love of violence, revengeful cruelty, fierce and implacable enmity" and the other things Augustine warned about. But I think the focus on the heart gets us closer to what is troubling about impersonal warfare. The flip side of robots' immunity to wrath or cruelty is that they also cannot feel empathy or show mercy to the enemy. They will carry out their programming with relentless, inexorable logic. That may make war more efficient and, in a sense, more rational, but it may also involve unnecessary killing when mercy might have been possible. It might bring a casual, unthinking, machine brutality to war where empathy might have prevailed (though critics will reply that unthinking brutality is not exactly novel to war, nor distinctive to robots).

Additionally, when something that was hard becomes easier, people are likely to do more of it. Because AI and robotics might make war more humane and less risky, they could make war easier and more frequent. Presidents and prime ministers will be more inclined to turn to lethal force—or will face less resistance to doing so—because they do not face the families of soldiers sent into harm's

[12] Scharre, *Army of None*, 287.

way, popular antiwar sentiment, Congressional opposition to large military deployments, and so forth. Push-button, robotic warfare carried out by our AI-powered soldier-servants could become an extremely tempting policy tool even when it is far from the last resort. And—to agree with part of Thacker's point above—it may become far easier to forget about the human cost on the other side of our robotic violence. With more psychological distance from the reality of war, commanders will find it easier to design and use the most efficient, most destructive, most lethal capabilities at their disposal.[13] When war is easy, life is cheap.

Israel has reportedly employed an artificially intelligent system, code-named "Lavender," to identify targets in its war against Hamas (see chapter 4). Before Lavender, human analysts undertook a labor-intensive process to "incriminate" a target by double-checking the intelligence that the target was, indeed, a member of Hamas. When Israel decided to expand its target list to include lower-ranking militants, it looked to Lavender to automate the lengthy process. As a result, "the role of human personnel in incriminating Palestinians as military operatives was pushed aside, and AI did most of the work instead." The AI was trained on data about existing Hamas militants: "It is fed data about existing Hamas operatives, it learns to notice their features" (like their social media profile, cell phone connections, and more) "and then it rates other Palestinians based on how similar they are to the militants." Human analysts reportedly double-checked Lavender's work, and once it had reached 90 percent accuracy, "the army authorized sweeping use of the system." Lavender became the de facto decision-maker: "If Lavender decided an individual was a

[13] See Scharre, 276.

militant in Hamas, [Israeli soldiers] were essentially asked to treat that as an order, with no requirement to independently check why the machine made that choice or to examine the raw intelligence data on which it is based." The report quotes one unnamed Israeli official commenting on Lavender: "The machine did it coldly. And that made it easier."[14]

Israel's system is a scaled-up, AI-enhanced version of the US's alleged past practice of "signature strikes," or targeting people "based on their behavior patterns and personal networks."[15] A signature strike is akin to convicting someone based on circumstantial evidence rather than eyewitness testimony or forensic data. In just war terms, it amounts to using different criteria for discrimination. In conventional war, we would distinguish between soldiers and civilians by seeing if they are wearing uniforms—or, more easily, if they are shooting at us. In the US's unconventional counterterrorism war, targeters reportedly discriminated militants from civilians by looking at their social profile; they did not wait to see who picked up a gun. Israel's Lavender AI takes the same approach at a much higher level. Signature strikes are surely more discriminating than World War II–era "area bombing," but that is a low bar. They are certainly less discriminating than precision-guided munitions aimed at confirmed targets—and any errors inherent in signature strikes will be magnified and multiplied when done at scale and at the speed of AI computing. Automated signature

---

[14] Yuval Abraham, "'Lavender': The AI Machine Directing Israel's Bombing Spree in Gaza," *+972 Magazine*, April 3, 2024, https://www.972mag.com/lavender-ai-israeli-army-gaza/.

[15] Micah Zenko, "Reforming U.S. Drone Strike Policies," Council on Foreign Relations, Special Report no. 654 (January 2013): vii, https://www.cfr.org/report/reforming-us-drone-strike-policies; see also 12–14.

strikes with little or no human oversight have extraordinary potential for error or abuse.[16]

There are still institutional checks that prevent democracies from casually resorting to robot war. But if even Israel, a democracy, so quickly and easily handed over decision-making authority to its AI, that leads us to the next risk: What kind of AI weapons will tyrants invent, and how will they use them? Almost every new technology is invented in good faith with visions for improving the human condition, and almost every new technology is hijacked by criminals, opportunists, and tyrants. Boston Dynamics claims on its website, "We will not authorize nor partner with those who wish to use our robots as weapons or autonomous targeting systems. If our products are being used for harm, we will take appropriate measures to mitigate that misuse."[17] That is commendable. But Boston Dynamics cannot control how its buyers will use its machines—nor how its competitors and emulators will market their products. The weaponization of robots like Atlas is inevitable. The nation that fields the first wave of autonomous soldiers, tanks, artillery, and jets will have an extraordinarily competitive edge in warfare.

Again, Boston Dynamics pledges itself to a long list of ethical guidelines, inviting transparency, obeying privacy laws, supporting regulation, and working with governments. "We believe that only people have the intelligence to manage the full complexity and richness of real-world conditions in our diverse places of work," they say.[18] But there are other AI developers with fewer scruples. Perhaps Russia or China will buy Atlas, reverse-engineer it, and remove all

---

[16] See Abraham, "'Lavender.'"

[17] "Boston Dynamics Ethical Principles," accessed September 9, 2024, https://bostondynamics.com/ethics/.

[18] "Boston Dynamics Ethical Principles."

the safety stops and ethical programming. It is a certainty that, somewhere, some corporation, government, or armed non-state group will find a way to invent an AI without ethical guidelines.

Then we will face the competitive pressure against a rival without the ethical restrictions we place on ourselves. What happens when we must fight a war against a nation armed with unconstrained AI? Will they have an advantage because of their willingness to fully entrust themselves to unshackled AI? Our systems—assuming we continue to abide by stringent guidelines—may operate more slowly and carefully because of human oversight, stricter regulation, and more programming restrictions. We will face competitive pressure either to loosen up or to risk losing.

The ultimate stakes are sobering. The plot of the 1964 film *Doctor Strangelove*—a bleak comedy satirizing the Cold War rivalry between the United States and the Soviet Union—turned on the existence of a Soviet "doomsday" or "dead hand" device, an automated nuclear counterstrike programmed to launch if the Soviet Union had been wiped out by American bombs. We learned decades later that the "dead hand" device was not wholly fictional.[19] A large portion of the world's nuclear weapons have already been under some form of automated command—and likely still are today. *Doctor Strangelove* ends, famously, when a rogue American nuclear strike hits the Soviet Union, triggering the dead hand and ending all life on earth.

Even short of nuclear Armageddon, all nations would be better off if each was assured that everyone had forsworn the most irresponsible forms of AI weaponry. As with every other form of arms control, everyone benefits if everyone cooperates to ban chemical

---

[19] See David E. Hoffman, *The Dead Hand: The Untold Story of the Cold Arms Race and Its Dangerous Legacy* (Palatine, IL: Anchor, 2009).

weapons, for example, or to limit intercontinental ballistic missiles. But it only takes one cheat to make everyone else vulnerable—and the awareness of that possibility makes it extremely tempting not to cooperate and, indeed, to be the first one to cheat. Finding a way to negotiate verifiable AI arms control and limitation may be the single most important policy initiative to keeping the twenty-first century livable.

Drones and Cyberwar

I want to return to the idea of push-button warfare because it is an issue that arises in other contexts besides artificial intelligence. Much of modern war is waged by, with, and through computers, remote sensors, drones, and other impersonal machinery. Again, this is good insofar as it allows one side, at least, not to risk human life. But the decrease in risk may make war too routine, to the point that presidents and prime ministers can push a button to cause death on the other side of the world as casually as they sign a law adjusting tax rates.

Some scholars have called for a new moral framework, *jus ad vim* ("just force"), to govern lethal violence below the threshold of war.[20] Such a framework would account for the lesser degree of violence involved in these small, surgical, computer-assisted strikes by relaxing the threshold that allows their use. We can use drones, for example, instead of going to war; and because they are comparatively cheap, less risky, and surgical, we can use them more often. In this view, *jus ad vim* would be a parallel set of criteria that mirrors the just war framework but with looser restrictions

---

[20] See Michael Walzer, *Just and Unjust Wars: A Moral Argument with Historical Illustrations*, 4th ed. (UK: Hachette, 2006), xv–xviii.

for smaller forms of violence, perhaps including assassination, riot control, counternarcotics, counterpiracy, and other operations that blur the line between law enforcement and combat.

I disagree. As I argued in chapter 3, the just war framework is a framework for any use of force—domestic and international, large and small. It is already the right framework for *jus ad vim.* If a government uses coercion, especially in a way that might take human life, it should be operating under the just war tradition. This is an important point to hold because this is what will keep the threshold for the use of force high even if and when the tools at our disposal become temptingly cheap, easy, and risk-free. President Obama warned about this dynamic in a 2013 speech. "The same human progress that gives us the technology to strike half a world away also demands the discipline to constrain that power—or risk abusing it," he said. "The very precision of drone strikes and the necessary secrecy often involved in such actions . . . can also lead a President and his team to view drone strikes as a cure-all for terrorism."[21]

President Obama was right (though I believe his actions did not match his words). To discipline the use of such tools, we have to see drone-bombing not as a different kind of policy to try before war. Drone-bombing *is* war carried out by different weapons, and that means it is permissible if and only if the criterion of last resort has already been met. We must meet that criterion before *any* military action, including drone strikes, is undertaken.

The same principle should apply to other unconventional tools, such as cyber operations that might kill humans. Most cyber operations—hacking computers, altering code, stealing information,

[21] Barack Obama, "Remarks by the President at the National Defense University," May 23, 2013, https://obamawhitehouse.archives.gov/the-press-office/2013/05/23/remarks-president-national-defense-university.

or planting viruses—are used by governments for espionage and sabotage (and by criminals for theft and vandalism) and fall outside the just war framework. But it is conceivable that a cyber operation could kill. It might shut off a power grid, depriving hospitals of electricity; sabotage air traffic control systems and cause planes to crash; or plant false military orders to an enemy unit, leading them directly into an ambush.

Again, such operations are push-button war: they are remote, mediated by machines, free of risk to human soldiers (on one side), and likely much easier and cheaper than conventional war. Yet such operations can kill. If they can kill—and especially if they are designed to kill—they should be governed by the same moral framework as any use of lethal force. Cyberwar, in particular, seems fraught. Many of the scenarios in which cyber-attacks could kill people—such as attacks on infrastructure—seem indiscriminate, even purposefully targeted at civilians. The ease of push-button warfare should not be an excuse for easy justification for killing, nor permission to relax the rules on whom to kill.

6

Pastoring Soldiers and Citizens in Wartime

Pastors and church leaders have an important role teaching their congregations how to think and pray about war and how to care for those who have participated in war. Some pastors may be wary of tackling the issue of war because it seems distant from the core mission of the church in preaching the gospel. But, as we discussed in chapter 2, doing justice is an integral part of the Bible's entire storyline. Part of the good news of the Bible is that God loves justice; we live in a universe in which the sovereign creator God cares about *mishpat* and *tzadeqah*. He wants to see people given their due, their rights respected, the rule of law followed, wrongs righted, right relationships restored, and communities flourishing under right ordering. Insofar as we love God and seek to emulate his character, we should love and do justice. The good news is that God empowers us through his Spirit to do so.

For most of us, most of the time, our opportunities to do justice are limited to ordering our homes, our churches, our workplaces, and our neighborhoods. But as citizens in a democracy, we have a small role to play in ordering our national life and even, through our elected government, in ordering the international system. In times of war, our voices and our deeds count. Our views on war are a way of showing the world what we mean when we talk about justice—and its Author. We show God's character when we speak about war and when we affirm the justice or injustice of the cause for which wars are fought or how wars are fought. Our deeds caring for those in war and after war are a way of showing the love of God. That is why church leaders have a responsibility to teach and lead their congregations to think and pray about war and to care for those involved in it.

Pastoring Soldiers, Veterans, and Widows and Orphans

The most immediate way churches minister in wartime is by caring for soldiers, veterans, and widows and orphans.

Soldiers

Soldiers deploying to war have a mess of emotions. I was sobered by the reality that I was going to war, excited to do something meaningful, afraid I might die, hopeful that I could make a difference, and afraid I would not get the chance. Soldiers closer to the front line than I ever was might feel anxious, not knowing if they will hold up under fire, be brave, stick by their comrades, and do their duty when danger presses close. Young men are likely to feel an urgent need to show that, yes, they are man enough: they can face death, walk through hell, confront the enemy, and return victorious. Being young men, they are also unlikely to articulate their feelings very well.

Pastors can counsel these soldiers in different ways. Those facing the possibility of death will always benefit from hearing the basic gospel message, a reassurance that Jesus will raise to new life those who turn from sin and trust in him. The resurrection can give courage to those paralyzed by fear of death, though some will need a reminder that dying in combat is not a Get Out of Jail Free card for unrepentant sin. But for soldiers carried away with the opposite feeling, with the desire to do something great or prove themselves, pastors can affirm the goodness of their service but remind them that the point is not their own glory but the cause of justice. Pastors should also remind soldiers that Jesus commands us to love our enemies. War tempts us to bloodlust and hatred, and young men easily get carried away when the shooting starts. Teaching about the just war tradition should help with these reminders, keeping soldiers focused on the justice of their cause rather than their personal glory, and on fighting with love for their enemies.

Because war can be an extreme trial and a time of suffering, it can also be an occasion for personal growth and spiritual maturity. "We rejoice in our sufferings, knowing that suffering produces endurance, and endurance produces character, and character produces hope" (Rom 5:3–4 ESV). Christian soldiers should "rejoice" if they suffer in war (fear, loneliness, and boredom as much as physical suffering from wounds) and look for the ways God can use suffering to produce character and virtue. That should help soldiers do their duty soberly and with courage, giving in to neither cowardice nor rashness. It is a difficult balance, but the best anchor in combat is the presence of others. It is a true cliché that soldiers fight less for a grand cause than for each other. Pastors should exhort soldiers to love their neighbors and make friends with other soldiers in their unit because those relationships will be the best support to help them overcome fear while keeping a spirit of selfless service. Others, in turn, may be drawn to Christians as combat approaches because of the calm hope Jesus gives. A Christian soldier's mere presence in a warzone should be a witness to the character and grace of God.

Veterans

Veterans returning from war face different challenges. One of my favorite bits from the movie trilogy *The Lord of the Rings* is a brief, wordless scene when the four hobbits return to the Shire after destroying the One Ring. They sit down at a pub, look around at the normal life everyone is leading—the idle conversation, friendly jesting, silly jokes, and laughter—and realize that no one had the slightest clue what danger and hell they had been through or what danger the world had been delivered from. The hobbits give each other a knowing, sad look.

Veterans may have lost friends in combat. They might have been wounded themselves. They may struggle with post-traumatic stress disorder (PTSD). Some veterans report feeling guilty for things they did or saw in combat. Many veterans feel bored by civilian life because it lacks the urgency, purposefulness, and structure of military life in wartime. If they had a "good war"—if they felt useful and supported the cause and came away feeling that their efforts made a difference for the better—they may be tempted to triumphalism. If they had a "bad war"—if they did not feel useful, became disillusioned with the cause, or felt their superiors made bad decisions that cost lives—they may feel bitterness or even despair. (Veterans commit suicide at higher rates than civilians.) Either way, veterans typically feel a sense of distance from civilians and an inability to communicate the reality of their experience. For years afterward, I felt isolated and lonely when the subject came up, and I resented what I felt was everyone else's neglect and ignorance of the war I served in.

Pastoring veterans in any of these circumstances can be challenging. Pastors may want to familiarize themselves with local resources for professional counseling, especially if a veteran is struggling with PTSD, suicidal thoughts, or feelings of depression or despair. But pastors have a unique role, even for those who need professional counseling. Pastors can and should walk with their congregants through grief, pain, guilt, boredom, bitterness, and everything else veterans may struggle with. Psalms and Lamentations are extraordinary guides to biblical grieving. And the Bible ends with a promise that God will make all things new, a promise that is profoundly good news to those who may feel broken, used up, or exhausted.

The gospel of Jesus is especially helpful for those who struggle with guilt. Some veterans may feel guilty because they are convicted that they made the wrong call, violated the principles of discrimination or proportionality, gave in to bloodlust, or used excessive force. They will need the help of their family, their church, and their pastors to walk through repentance, discern what restitution could look like, and hear the good news of God's mercy.

Others may feel guilty because they do not know if they did the right thing. The fog and uncertainty of combat often makes it hard to know exactly what happened, who was responsible for what, or if a judgment call was the right one, especially if information later comes to light casting doubt on decisions made in the moment. Similarly, some veterans experience "moral injury" (psychological harm to one's conscience) after killing another human being, even in clearly justified circumstances. These veterans would benefit from a pastor's help, perhaps alongside other soldiers, to walk through their experiences and recount their decisions. The just war tradition should reassure them that, as we are to love our enemies, it is appropriate to grieve the enemy's death, a practice that many soldiers today are likely unfamiliar with yet one that could go a long way toward healing the psychological scars of war. God reminds us that he has "no pleasure in the death of the wicked" (Ezek 33:11). But the just war tradition should also remind us that the work of defending peace and justice is necessary and commendable. We can mourn the necessity of war and yet give honor to those who carry it out.[1]

Encouraging veterans to speak to pastors and fellow soldiers can also help, not so much to establish if their decisions were right or wrong but to ease their worry and doubt by simply telling the story out loud to others. Judgment calls made in the stress and confusion of combat are just that—judgment calls—and should not be measured by the same standard by which we measure later historical accounts made with the full knowledge of the facts. But for veterans, their feeling of guilt can grow simply because we keep things to ourselves, and the longer we do not share, the more it comes to seem like a secret that should be kept hidden. Pastors can help veterans tell their story to their church family.

Pastors and church families can also help veterans feel proud of their service, especially for those who may feel embittered or think their service was fruitless. Many churches include prayers and expressions of gratitude for servicemen and servicewomen around Memorial Day, Independence Day, and other American holidays. That is fine (though churches will always want to be careful not to conflate American and Christian identity).[2] But routine public

---

[1] For more on moral injury and just war, see Marc LiVecche, *The Good Kill: Just War and Moral Injury* (UK: Oxford Univ. Press, 2021).

[2] For a longer discussion of the relationship between Christianity and America, see Paul D. Miller, *The Religion of American Greatness: What's Wrong with Christian Nationalism* (Downers Grove, IL: InterVarsity, 2022).

expressions like that do not quite speak to the individual who may feel conflicted about his or her service. Pastors can remind veterans that God values our secular vocations, that all work is sanctified to him. All work is marred by the fall and prone to be frustrated by sin and foolishness. Nonetheless, "whatever your hands find to do, do with all your strength" (Eccl 9:10). As Paul encourages us, "Whatever you do, do it from the heart, as something done for the Lord and not for people" (Col 3:23). Veterans can and should be proud of service done in honesty and good faith, to defend justice and peace, regardless of its outcome in this world.

Widows and Orphans

War kills people, which means war leaves behind broken families and grieving loved ones. The care of widows and orphans was one of the first and most distinctive ministries of the early church, and it should still be today: "Pure and undefiled religion before God the Father is this: to look after orphans and widows in their distress and to keep oneself unstained from the world" (Jas 1:27). Families need help grieving lost ones and finding hope on the other side of grief. They will want to share memories and talk of their lost loved ones with people who knew them. American evangelicalism, focused on seeker-sensitive and market-driven growth strategies, has often overlooked biblical lamentation and sorrow. All Christians have cause to grieve, but it does not always come naturally. Pastors will have to shepherd people through what may be an unfamiliar spiritual discipline.[3]

[3] For an excellent introduction to biblical grieving, see Mark Vroegop, *Dark Clouds, Deep Mercy: Discovering the Grace of Lament* (Wheaton, IL: Crossway, 2019).

Single parents will have myriad practical needs raising children, working, and—for many of them, eventually—looking for another spouse. They are likely to need financial assistance. They may need help navigating the difficult bureaucracies—the Department of Veterans Affairs and the Social Security Administration—that afford public benefits to widows and widowers. Children will need other adults to step in to help with discipleship and mentoring, as appropriate to their age level. Churches that already have ministries for the poor, the homeless, or immigrants will find substantial overlap between those groups' needs and the needs of widows and orphans. Churches that lack such ministries may want to start them.

Pastoring Citizens, Taxpayers, and Voters

In a democracy, every citizen is involved in decisions about war and peace. Though most of us are not giving advice to the president or making strategic decisions, our voice counts at the ballot box and in public opinion polls. Presidents regularly consult polls to guide their decisions, even in national security affairs. (Whether they should is another matter, but they certainly do.) Through our votes, our tax dollars, and our civic engagement, we are part of the process of going to war, fighting war, and ending wars well.

Pastors should speak to their congregations about the regular responsibility that all citizens have to be informed, get involved, and advocate for justice. As always, doing justice in the world is not the main point of the gospel—Jesus did not come to sanctify our political advocacy—but the desire to do justice is and should be a primary outworking of gospel-changed lives. As citizens with a unique opportunity to do justice by advocating for the just use of force and for just limitations on it, we have a responsibility to use that privilege well.

That means, first, staying reasonably well-informed about the wars we fight or that we may become involved in. This is harder than it sounds. Americans watch an extraordinary amount of television (and YouTube and TikTok), including news and commentary, and we *feel* well-informed—which makes it harder to recognize how ignorant we really are. Americans would be more responsible citizens if we stopped watching TV and using social media altogether and at least admitted how ignorant we are about most things in the world. Televisual media (including most of the internet) is shallow and does not convey much informational content; it relies on images and emotions and, again, makes the viewers feel as if we have learned or experienced something when we have, in fact, merely passively watched it.[4]

To be informed means engaging with facts. Written media—newspapers, magazines, journals, and books—are far more informationally dense and emotionally dispassionate. Of course, they can be just as partisan and biased, but the nature of the written word means we are more actively engaged—the neurons in our brains literally show more electrical activity when reading than when watching TV. We are required to *think* about what we are reading, which makes us participants in education rather than consumers of content. Citizens, voters, and taxpayers should read. If we are fighting a war, we should read about the war. If we are close to intervening in

[4] See Jonathan Haidt, "Why the Past 10 Years of American Life Have Been Uniquely Stupid," *Atlantic*, May 2022, https://www.theatlantic.com/magazine/archive/2022/05/social-media-democracy-trust-babel/629369/; see also Neil Postman, *Amusing Ourselves to Death: Public Discourse in the Age of Show Business* (New York: Penguin, 2005).

a war—as we are in Ukraine and Israel—we should read about that too. Allowing our leaders to take us to war and not caring enough to stay informed about it—as was the case during the long war in Afghanistan—is a dereliction of our duties as citizens.

Reading and getting informed is the necessary prelude to the most important part of our civic duty: voting and advocacy. When we vote for a candidate, we are exercising power on behalf of a vision of justice that the candidate or party represents. Sadly, any vision of justice represented by an earthly political party or sinful human being is necessarily partial, flawed, and mixed with injustice. When we vote, we typically must pick the lesser of two injustices or vote strategically based on our understanding of the balance of power between rival parties across the branches of government.[5] That is true generally of all public issues, including foreign policy, diplomacy, war, and peace.

Some things should be obvious: Christians should not vote for candidates or parties that advocate war crimes or murder. Christians should not vote for candidates or parties that advocate for international aggression, wars of conquest or glory, ethnic cleansing, and so forth. Fortunately, such clear-cut cases are rare. Parties and candidates typically spin their agendas to make it sound good because they know voters want to feel like they are the good guys. No one comes right out and says, "Vote for evil." Just as Satan comes disguised as an angel of light, wicked political ideologies come speaking the language of justice and peace. That makes it harder, but more important, to exercise judgment and discern where the balance of justice lies between rival candidates and parties.

[5] For example, I have a strong preference for voting for divided government so that no single party controls all branches.

I suggest a general rule of thumb both for voting and for our own hearts: recognize the most dangerous temptation we face, and try to exhibit, and vote for, the opposite. In wartime, the most dangerous temptation is bloodlust, vengeance, cruelty, and triumphalism, so we should advocate and vote for the measured, dispassionate, and necessary use of force until victory, and then advocate for magnanimity and charity in the aftermath. Vote for candidates who seem to exhibit a mature attitude toward the use of force in wartime: neither triumphalist nor defeatist, committed to victory but not vengeance. "I am tired and sick of war. Its glory is all moonshine," General William Tecumseh Sherman lamented. "It is only those who have neither fired a shot nor heard the shrieks and groans of the wounded who cry aloud for blood, for vengeance, for desolation."[6] Sherman, who served in the Union army during the American Civil War, was a victorious general in a just war. Yet he famously concluded, "War is hell." That's the attitude we should want our presidents to have.[7]

In peacetime, the most dangerous temptation is functional pacifism, a naïve utopianism that argues war cannot or will not recur, that any talk of war or military preparation is irresponsible warmongering. Many of my students over the years were functional pacifists—not convictional pacifists in the Amish or Mennonite tradition, which I can respect, but pacifists through an unreflective

[6] See William T. Sherman, Civil War | Biography, American Battlefield Trust website, accessed May 7, 2024, https://www.battlefields.org/learn/biographies/william-t-sherman.

[7] The quote is usually presented as one contiguous quote from a single source. In fact, the first part comes from an 1865 letter, but the conclusion—"war is hell"—is from an 1879 commencement address. Sherman did say everything in the quote, but not together. History has merged them together—for the better, I think.

attitude that disdained the military, assumed without evidence that diplomacy would always be sufficient to meet international challenges, and implicitly believed no one would be irrational enough to start another war.

The problem with functional pacifism is that it tends to lead to wild swings in popular sentiment. If you think war will never recur and then another 9/11 happens or China invades Taiwan, you are likely to overreact. Functional pacifism evaporated instantly on 9/11, sometimes giving way to overheated passion. Then it reemerged around 2005, when disillusionment with the war in Iraq started growing. It instantly disappeared again in February 2022, when Russia invaded Ukraine. I was surprised that some of my students who, in the years after Iraq, saw little reason to care about military affairs, suddenly advocated direct military intervention against Russia in the days after its invasion of Ukraine. They went from pacifism to cheerleaders for World War III within hours. We should advocate and vote for prudent, cautious, level-headed military preparation in peacetime to deter wars from breaking out in the first place and to be prepared to fight and win if they do.

One final thought on our responsibilities as citizens and taxpayers. We should support close oversight and expect high moral standards of our armies. It is not unpatriotic to scrutinize how we fight, to ensure we are fighting justly, to investigate and, if necessary, hold military leaders and individual soldiers accountable for war crimes and abuses. Indeed, we should be unsurprised when such crimes happen. Our armies are made up of sinners—some redeemed, some not, but all prone to the same temptations that soldiers have always faced. Some will give in. In 1968, US Army soldiers murdered hundreds of Vietnamese civilians in what came to be known as the My Lai massacre. In 2004, more soldiers were found to be complicit in systematic abuses of Iraqi prisoners at the

Abu Ghraib prison complex. Those are just the better known and better documented instances in recent American military history. Every military's history is replete with such accounts; the Russian military, for example, is notorious for making such abuses a deliberate part of its strategy to terrorize civilian populations. Holding our armies accountable by supporting Congress's oversight role and protecting the work of inspectors general is an important way citizens can ensure we fight justly.

Pastoring Decision-Makers

Some pastors have the responsibility to counsel political decision-makers. While all citizens share in decision-making in a democracy, some play a more direct role. I have attended churches in the Washington, DC, area for most of my adult life. Generals and admirals, political appointees, and members of Congress are often in the pews. How should pastors shepherd them?

First, pastors should reread Jas 2:2–4:

> For if someone comes into your meeting wearing a gold ring and dressed in fine clothes, and a poor person dressed in filthy clothes also comes in, if you look with favor on the one wearing the fine clothes and say, "Sit here in a good place," and yet you say to the poor person, "Stand over there," or "Sit here on the floor by my footstool," haven't you made distinctions among yourselves and become judges with evil thoughts?

James's warning against showing favoritism to the rich applies just as well to the powerful. Pastors should not modify their preaching to please powerful people in the pews or to avoid offending them. Powerful people need to hear the unvarnished, uncompromising

Word of God just as much as the rest of us—indeed, they probably need it more. If it is hard for a rich man to enter the kingdom of heaven, it is likely just as hard for a powerful man to do so. Jesus's warning applies to everyone with any form of the world's wealth, including power (and fame, beauty, and intelligence).

Second, policymakers especially need to hear about the requirement of right intention. As those most directly responsible for war, they will be held to account before God for the decisions they make and the condition of their hearts as they make them. The just war tradition was originally formulated by theologians and priests to speak to the princes and knights under their pastoral care. The exhortation to fight in good faith with genuine concern for peace and justice—not as a pretext for an ulterior motive, such as vengeance or glory—and to fight without hatred are as relevant today as they have ever been. In my view, recent American history has shown policymakers from both parties generally failing to follow through on their professions of right intention—failing to invest in lasting order, justice, and conciliation in wars' aftermath.

Third, policymakers need to be reminded that we will "recognize them by their fruit" (Matt 7:16). Policymakers may claim they have right intention, but their actual wartime decisions will show the fruit of what is in their hearts. And their hearts will be laid bare. In this life, policymakers often appeal to the "verdict of history" to justify their decisions, especially unpopular ones—and, indeed, historians' work in subsequent generations often unearths memos, letters, and diaries that bring to light policymakers' thought processes and cast doubt on the claims they made in the moment. But even if later historians vindicate policymakers, policymakers still face a more important test: "For nothing is concealed that won't be revealed, and nothing hidden that won't be made known and brought to light" (Luke 8:17). Pastors should lovingly remind policymakers that they will be held to account in this life and the next.

Policymakers may also need encouragement. War never goes according to plan; there are always setbacks and unexpected turns. Every wartime leader and decision-maker faces extraordinary scrutiny and criticism. Leaders may quail and begin to doubt their cause or their strategy. While pastors are not best positioned to give strategic advice—they can comment on the morality, not the effectiveness, of strategy—they should give encouragement to persevere in a just cause. If a war is just, it is just to win; and that means it is just to keep going in the face of the enemy's violence and critics' complaints. That does not mean policymakers should never review their policy and strategy to assess their effectiveness, only that a singular focus on justice and peace—which pastors can help with—can help policymakers see their way through obstacles. There is a "moral imperative of victory" in a just war, of which policymakers may lose sight in the complexity, confusion, and self-doubt of wartime.[8]

Pastors' final exhortation to policymakers should be a reminder of General Sherman's maxim: "War is hell." Long before Sherman, Augustine argued that this may be iconographically true, in a theological sense: war is an icon of hell itself. For Augustine, the true horror of war was not merely bodily harm and suffering but the inner torment of conflict, which he understood to be the state of souls in hell. Just as the final state of the just is heavenly peace, the final state of the wicked—i.e., hell—is a kind of never-ending

---

[8] Pauline Shanks Kaurin, "Necessity, Convenience, and Point of View," in *Military Necessity and Just War Statecraft: The Principle of National Security Stewardship*, ed. Eric Patterson and Marc LiVecche (New York: Routledge, 2023).

experience of the horrors of war. Just as the rightly ordered city is an icon of the city of God and the heavenly paradise that awaits the just, the state of war is an icon of hell, the just punishment of the damned.[9] The only thing worse than hell is a universe without God; similarly, the only thing worse than war is a world without justice.

If war is an icon of hell, we should fervently shun war and hate it. This book is premised on the idea that war can, sometimes, be just—yet history shows that most wars are not. Even wars that are more just than not always come mixed with injustice—in the motives of leaders, the hearts of soldiers, the means of fighting, or (almost always) the imperfect aftermath. We should seek every means possible to avoid war. When serving as assistant secretary of the Navy in 1918, Franklin Roosevelt traveled to France and toured the trenches of the worst war the world had yet seen. Years later he reflected on the experience:

> I have seen war. I have seen war on land and sea. I have seen blood running from the wounded. I have seen men coughing out their gassed lungs. I have seen the dead in the mud. I have seen cities destroyed. I have seen two hundred limping, exhausted men come out of line—the survivors of a regiment of one thousand that went forward forty-eight hours before. I have seen children starving. I have seen the agony of mothers and wives. I hate war.[10]

Recall the psalmist's condemnation of the man who has "war . . . in his heart" (Ps 55:21). Let us hate war, and teach that hatred.

---

[9] See Augustine, *City of God Against the Pagans*, ed. R. W. Dyson (Cambridge, UK: Cambridge Univ. Press, 1998), 962.

[10] Franklin D. Roosevelt, "Address at Chautauqua, N.Y.," August 14, 1936, https://www.presidency.ucsb.edu/node/208921.

Hating war is how we love our neighbors, even when we must fight. Hating war is also how we love our enemies, *especially* when we fight. Only if we truly hate war will we fight as a last resort, fight only for a just cause, fight with respect for the human dignity of our enemies and allies alike, and seek to repair the damage of war in the aftermath.

SELECTED BIBLIOGRAPHY

Abraham, Yuval. "'Lavender': The AI Machine Directing Israel's Bombing Spree in Gaza." *+972 Magazine*, April 3, 2024. https://www.972mag.com/lavender-ai-israeli-army-gaza/.

Aquinas, Thomas. *On Law, Morality, and Politics.* Edited by William P. Baumgarth and Richard J. Regan. Indianapolis, IN: Hackett, 1988.

Asimov, Isaac. *I. Robot.* New York: HarperVoyager, 2013.

Augustine, *The City of God Against the Pagans.* Edited by R. W. Dyson. UK: Cambridge Univ. Press, 1998.

Bainton, Roland H. "The Early Church and War." *Harvard Theological Review* 39, no. 3 (1946): 189–212.

Charles, J. Daryl, and Timothy J. Demy. *War, Peace, and Christianity: Questions and Answers from a Just-War Perspective.* Wheaton, IL: Crossway, 2010.

Churchill, Winston. "Their Finest Hour," June 18, 1940. https://winstonchurchill.org/resources/speeches/1940-the-finest-hour/their-finest-hour/.

Clines, D. J. A. "The Image of God in Man." *Tyndale Bulletin* 19, no. 1 (1968): 53–103. https://www.tyndalebulletin.org/article/30671-the-image-of-god-in-man.

Confucius, *The Analects of Confucius.* Translated by Arthur Waley. New York: Vintage, 1989.

Deane, Herbert A. *The Political and Social Ideas of St. Augustine.* New York: Columbia Univ. Press, 1963.

ESV Study Bible. Wheaton, IL: Crossway, 2008.

Fabian, Emmanuel. "Defense Minister Announces 'Complete Siege' of Gaza." *Times of Israel*, October 9, 2023. https://www.timesofisrael.com/liveblog_entry/defense-minister-announces-complete-siege-of-gaza-no-power-food-or-fuel/.

Foner, Eric. *The Fiery Trial: Abraham Lincoln and American Slavery.* New York: Norton, 2011.

Fukuyama, Francis. "The End of History?" *National Interest* (Summer 1989): 3–18. https://pages.ucsd.edu/~bslantchev/courses/pdf/Fukuyama%20-%20End%20of%20History.pdf.

Ganguly, K. M., trans. *Mahabharata Anusasana Parva.* https://www.mahabharataonline.com/translation/mahabharata_13b078.php.

Haidt, Jonathan. "Why the Past 10 Years of American Life Have Been Uniquely Stupid." *Atlantic*, May 2022. https://www.theatlantic.com/magazine/archive/2022/05/social-media-democracy-trust-babel/629369/.

Hauerwas, Stanley. *War and the American Difference: Theological Reflections on Violence and National Identity.* Grand Rapids: Baker Academic, 2011.

Hobbes, Thomas. *Leviathan.* Edited by Edwin Curley. Indianapolis, IN: Hackett, 1994.

Hoffman, Bruce. "Understanding Hamas's Genocidal Intent." *Atlantic*, October 10, 2023. https://www.theatlantic.com/international/archive/2023/10/hamas-covenant-israel-attack-war-genocide/675602/.

Hoffman, David E. *The Dead Hand: The Untold Story of the Cold War Arms Race and Its Dangerous Legacy.* Palatine, IL: Anchor, 2009.

Holladay, William L., ed. *A Concise Hebrew and Aramaic Lexicon of the Old Testament*. Grand Rapids: Eerdmans, 1971.

Holmes, Arthur. *War and Christian Ethics*. Grand Rapids: Baker Academic, 2005.

"Joint Soviet-United States Statement on the Summit Meeting in Geneva." November 21, 1985. Ronald Reagan Presidential Library and Museum. https://www.reaganlibrary.gov/archives/speech/joint-soviet-united-states-statement-summit-meeting-geneva.

Justinian. *Justinian Institutes*. https://gutenberg.org/cache/epub/5983/pg5983-images.html.

Kagan, Robert. *The Ghost at the Feast: America and the Collapse of World Order, 1900–1941*. Vol. 2. New York: Vintage, 2024.

Kaurin, Pauline Shanks. "Necessity, Convenience, and Point of View." In *Military Necessity and Just War Statecraft: The Principle of National Security Stewardship*. Edited by Eric Patterson and Marc LiVecche. New York: Routledge, 2023.

Keller, Timothy. *Generous Justice: How God's Grace Makes Us Just*. New York: Penguin, 2012.

Kelly, John Norman Davidson. *Early Christian Doctrines*. London: A&C Black, 2000.

Kroenig, Matthew. *The Return of Great Power Rivalry: Democracy Versus Autocracy from the Ancient World to the US and China*. New York: Oxford Univ. Press, 2020.

Lasswell, Harold D. *Politics: Who Gets What, When, How*. Tauranga, NZ: Papamoa, 2018.

Leeman, Jonathan. *How the Nations Rage: Rethinking Faith and Politics in a Divided Age*. Nashville, TN: Thomas Nelson, 2018.

———. *Political Church: The Local Assembly as Embassy of Christ's Rule*. Downers Grove, IL: InterVarsity, 2016.

Lewis, C. S. *The Abolition of Man*. Grand Rapids: Zondervan, 2001.

Liddell, Henry George and Robert Scott. *Greek-English Lexicon*, 9th ed. New York: Oxford Univ. Press, 1996.

LiVecche, Marc. *The Good Kill: Just War and Moral Injury*. UK: Oxford Univ. Press, 2021.

Machiavelli, Niccolo. *The Prince*. Translated by Luigi Ricci. New York: New American Library, 1952.

Maizland, Lindsay. "Why China-Taiwan Relations Are So Tense." *Council on Foreign Relations* (2024). https://www.cfr.org/backgrounder/china-taiwan-relations-tension-us-policy-biden.

Masters, Jonathan. "Ukraine: Conflict at the Crossroads of Europe and Russia." *Council on Foreign Relations* (2023). https://www.cfr.org/backgrounder/ukraine-conflict-crossroads-europe-and-russia.

Miller, Paul. "The Unreality of Realism in International Relations." H-DIPLO | ISSF Essay 49, October 2, 2019. https://issforum.org/essays/49-realism.

Miller, Paul D. *American Power and Liberal Order: A Conservative Internationalist Grand Strategy*. Washington, DC: Georgetown Univ. Press, 2016.

———. *Just War and Ordered Liberty*. New York: Cambridge Univ. Press, 2021.

———. *The Religion of American Greatness: What's Wrong with Christian Nationalism*. Downers Grove, IL: InterVarsity, 2022.

Murray, John. *Principles of Conduct: Aspects of Biblical Ethics*. Grand Rapids: Eerdmans, 1957.

Niditch, Susan. *War in the Hebrew Bible: A Study in the Ethics of Violence*. New York: Oxford Univ. Press, 1995.

Nixon, Richard. "Transcript of David Frost's Interview with Richard Nixon," 1977. https://teachingamericanhistory.org/document/transcript-of-david-frosts-interview-with-richard-nixon/.

Padget, Timothy. *Swords and Ploughshares: American Evangelicals on War, 1937, 1973*. Bellingham, WA: Lexham, 2018.

Patterson, Eric. *A Basic Guide to the Just War Tradition*. Grand Rapids: Baker, 2023.

———. "Military Necessity, Proportionality, and Discrimination." In *The Ethics of Urban Warfare: City and War*. Edited by Dragan Stanar and Kristina Tom. Boston, MA: Brill, 2023.

———. *Ending Wars Well: Order, Justice, and Conciliation in Contemporary Post-Conflict*. New Haven, CT: Yale Univ. Press, 2012.

———, and J. Daryl Charles, eds. *Just War and Christian Traditions*. Notre Dame, IN: Univ. of Notre Dame Press, 2022.

Postman, Neil. *Amusing Ourselves to Death: Public Discourse in the Age of Show Business*. New York: Penguin, 2005.

Preston, Andrew. *Sword of the Spirit, Shield of Faith: Religion in American War and Diplomacy*. Toronto: Knopf, 2012.

Ramsey, Paul. *The Just War: Force and Political Responsibility*. Lanham, MD: Rowman & Littlefield, 2002.

———. *War and the Christian Conscience*. Whitefish, MT: Literary Licensing, 2011.

Reagan, Ronald. "Address to Members of the British Parliament." June 8, 1982. https://www.reaganlibrary.gov/archives/speech/address-members-british-parliament.

Roberts, Andrew, James Donaldson, and A. Cleveland Coxe, eds. *Ante-Nicene Fathers, Vol 1*. Translated by Alexander Roberts and James Donaldson. Buffalo, New York: Christian Literature

Publishing, 1885. Revised and edited for *New Advent* by Kevin Knight. http://www.newadvent.org/fathers/0101.htm.

Roosevelt, Franklin D. "Address at Chautauqua, NY." August 14, 1936. https://www.presidency.ucsb.edu/node/208921.

Rosenberg, Yair. "What Did Israeli Top Officials Really Say About Gaza?" *Atlantic*, January 21, 2024. https://www.theatlantic.com/international/archive/2024/01/israel-south-africa-genocide-case-fake-quotes/677198/.

Rowen, Herbert H. "'L'Etat c'est Moi': Louis XIV and the State." *French Historical Studies* 2, no. 1 (1961): 83–98. https://doi.org/10.2307/286184.

Ruyter, Knut Willem. "Pacifism and Military Service in the Early Church." *CrossCurrents* 32, no. 1 (1982): 54–70.

Sarotte, Mary Elise, "A Broken Promise?" *Foreign Affairs* (September/October 2014). https://www.foreignaffairs.com/articles/russia-fsu/2014-08-11/broken-promise.

Scharre, Paul. *Army of None: Autonomous Weapons and the Future of War*. New York: Norton, 2018.

Schmitt, Michael N., and John J. Merriam. "The Tyranny of Context: Israeli Targeting Practices in Legal Perspective." *University of Pennsylvania Journal of International Law* 37 (2015): 53–138.

Schreiner, Thomas R. *The King in His Beauty: A Biblical Theology of the Old and New Testaments*. Grand Rapids: Baker, 2013.

Shean, John F. *Soldiering for God: Christianity and the Roman Army*. Vol. 61. Boston: Brill, 2010.

Smith, Charles. *Palestine and the Arab-Israeli Conflict,* 10th ed. Bedford, NY: St. Martin's, 2020.

Stanar, Dragan and Kristina Tom, eds. *The Ethics of Urban Warfare: City and War*. Vol. 10. Boston: Brill, 2022.

Stout, Harry S. *Upon the Altar of the Nation: A Moral History of the Civil War*. New York: Penguin, 2007.

Tacitus. "Agricola 30.4." In Morely, Neville. *The Roman Empire: Roots of Imperialism*, 38–69. London: Pluto, 2010. Epigraph.

Tertullian, *De Corona*. Translated by S. Thelwall. From *Ante-Nicene Fathers*, Vol. 3. Edited by Alexander Roberts, James Donaldson, and A. Cleveland Coxe. Buffalo, NY: Christian Literature Publishing, 1885. Revised and edited for *New Advent* by Kevin Knight. http://www.newadvent.org/fathers/0304.htm.

Thacker, Jason. *The Age of AI: Artificial Intelligence and the Future of Humanity*. Grand Rapids: Zondervan, 2020.

Thucydides, *History*. Translated by Rex Warner. Edited by M. I. Finley. New York: Penguin, 1954.

VanDrunen, David. *Natural Law: A Short Companion*. Brentwood, TN: B&H Academic, 2023.

———. *Natural Law and the Two Kingdoms: A Study in the Development of Reformed Social Thought*. Grand Rapids: Eerdmans, 2009.

———. *Politics after Christendom: Political Theology in a Fractured World*. Grand Rapids: Zondervan Academic, 2020.

Vroegop, Mark. *Dark Clouds, Deep Mercy: Discovering the Grace of Lament*. Wheaton, IL: Crossway, 2019.

Waltke, Bruce K., and Ivan D. V. De Silva. *Proverbs: A Shorter Commentary*. Grand Rapids: Eerdmans, 2021.

Waltz, Kenneth N. "Nuclear Myths and Political Realities." *American Political Science Review* 84, no. 3 (1990): 731–45. https://doi.org/10.2307/1962764.

Walzer, Michael. *Just and Unjust Wars: A Moral Argument with Historical Illustrations*, 4th ed. New York: Basic Books, 2006.

Wilken, Robert Louis. *Liberty in the Things of God: The Christian Origin of Religious Freedom*. New Haven, CT: Yale Univ. Press, 2019.

Winters, Francis X. *Remembering Hiroshima: Was it Just?* New York: Routledge, 2016.

Wolterstorff, Nicholas. *Justice: Rights and Wrongs*. Princeton, NJ: Princeton Univ. Press, 2008.

Yoder, John Howard. *Nevertheless: The Varieties and Shortcomings of Religious Pacifism*. Huntington, IN: Herald, 1992.

Zenko, Micah. "Reforming U.S. Drone Strike Policies." *Council on Foreign Relations*, Special Report No. 654 (January 2013): vii. See also pp. 12–14. https://www.cfr.org/report/reforming-us-drone-strike-policies.

SUBJECT INDEX

P

Q

R

S

SCRIPTURE INDEX